Python Programming and GUIs

for Electronic Engineers

Andrew Pratt

Python Programming and GUIs

for Electronic Engineers

Andrew Pratt

Elektor International Media BV
P.O. Box 11
6114 ZG Susteren
The Netherlands

British Library Cataloguing in Publication Data
A catalogue record for this book is available from the British Library

ISBN 978-0-905705-87-3

Prepress production: Kontinu, Sittard
Design cover: Helfrich Ontwerpbureau, Deventer
First published in the United Kingdom 2010
Printed in the Netherlands by Wilco, Amersfoort
© Elektor International Media BV 2010

109012-UK

Table of Contents

Preface

This book is intended to be a practical guide to interfacing simple hardware projects with a PC. There are many topics covered in the book. They are specifically included in order to achieve the aim of communicating with a particular interface device, the latter chosen for its availability and low cost.

The interface device used herein is the UM245 by Future Technologies Development International (FTDI). This is a development module that is supplied with an FT245 chip on a circuit board with a USB socket. This allows the engineer to read and write to 8 inputs/outputs. The current price of the UM245 is around twelve pounds in the UK. It is possible to communicate with more than one of these devices.

By the end of the book you will be able to control hardware from your own desktop graphic user interface (GUI) or from a web browser on the other side of the world over the Internet. To do this the book will explain how to program in python, write web pages, setup an apache web server, and write 'server side' code. Some simple electronic circuits will be presented to give your software applications something to drive. These will be limited to turning lights on and off, accepting input from switches or from an analogue to digital converter.

Also an introduction to Linux is given as accompanied in the form of a CD which can be downloaded. This CD is used to boot up your computer into an operating system that is independent of your existing system which offers a safe programming environment that cannot harm your existing hard drive. This CD contains all the software tools you need for the exercises in the book.

It should be appreciated that none of the topics are covered in utmost depth, however enough information is provided to achieve the aim and give the reader a start in each of these. Each chapter introducing a new topic will not cover everything in that chapter. Subsequent chapters will add to those topics as required.

It is assumed the reader is familiar with using a computer but no knowledge of programming is expected. A basic knowledge of electricity and discrete electronic components such as resistors, switches, and LEDs is required and the ability to solder simple components and wires together.

Chapter 1

Linux

1.1 Introduction

Linux has been chosen as the operating system because, as you will see as you read the book, you have so much freedom to change things and experiment. The version of Linux described here is what is called a "live" or bootable distribution. This means the computer will boot up from a CD or a USB memory stick and a virtual drive will be created in the computer's memory. This virtual drive, together with its file system, will only exist while the computer is running; the data and the operating system on your existing hard drive will not be affected.

To get round the obvious problem of losing any work you create, a memory stick can be "mounted" on to this virtual file system and data saved to it. If you are already a Linux user and have it installed on your computer you can still use the bootable disk. I would recommend using the live distribution as all the necessary software applications are already installed and configured and the whole system is completely portable from one computer to another.

1.2 Getting the CD

The first thing you need is a fairly modern computer running a Pentium processor or better, a CD ROM writer and 256 Mbytes of RAM. The CD can be obtained by downloading from the www.elektor.com support page related to this book. A broadband internet connection will be required as the CD is nearly 300MBytes. What you are downloading is a large file known as an image. This image has to be burned onto a real CD. It will not work if you just copy the image file to the CD, you have to select the option on your CD writing software to "burn CD image". The exact details will depend on the CD writing software being used.

1.3 Booting Linux

To boot your computer from the CD you might need to alter the BIOS settings to put the

CD ROM drive above your hard drive in the boot order. This requires you to press a key on the keyboard as the computer is initially starting, the key required is shown on the screen with a message such as "press Del to setup" or similar.

Once you are in the BIOS menus find the boot order menu and follow the instructions to change the order and save the settings. Again the details will depend on your computer.

Now you can boot the computer up into this version of Linux, which is called Slax a distribution based on Slackware. The CD you have got has been re-mastered from the standard Slax CD to include the software applications needed to write your own software and interface with the FTDI chip. To find out more about Slax you can visit "http://slax.org". Chapter 11 will deal with creating your own customized Linux live CD.

1.4 Finding Your Way Round

If you are new to Linux things are going to seem strange at first, particularly the file directories. Also if you are new to live distributions you are going to get used to the fact that the basic file system is only in memory. Throughout the book we are going to be using the command line to access files, start applications etc. This might seem like a backward step if you remember the old DOS days, but the Linux command line is full of quick short cuts and time saving tricks. Also while writing programs the same command line statements will sometimes need to be put into the code.

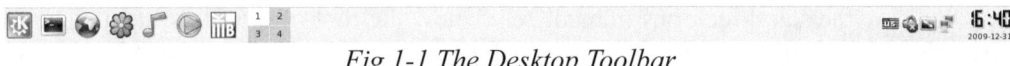
Fig 1-1 The Desktop Toolbar

Fig 1-1 shows the desktop toolbar after bootup. Slax is a fully featured operating system that you can use for normal "click and drag" domestic computing. To get started, click on the black Terminal Program icon on the left of the tool bar. Fig1-2 shows the command line interface known as a console, I have squashed it here to save space.

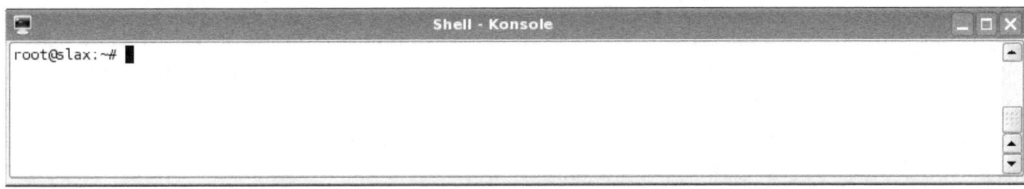
Fig 1-2

This figure shows that we are in our home directory, the "~" means home directory. This is the home directory of the system administrator known as root, hence root@slax: As an introduction to the command line type "cd /" without the " ". Press return, then type "ls" and press return. The result is shown below, directories show up in blue with a "/" after their names implying that there might be subdirectories. From now on command line commands will be included in the book's texts inline not as a figure. Note that Linux is case sensitive commands are lower case. For a file name "File.txt" would be a different file from "file.txt"

root@slax:~# cd /
root@slax:/# ls
bin/ boot/ dev/ etc/ home/ lib/ mnt/ opt/ proc/ root/ sbin/ srv/ sys/ tmp/ usr/ var/
root@slax:/#

Please note that the keyboard has been configured for the American layout. If you want to change it right click on the American flag logo and choose your country. If it's not on that list left click on the configure item and add the country you want.

It's now time to clear up a point that might otherwise cause confusion. You are "root". You have a home directory called root that you can see in the list above. All of the directories in this figure are the first sub-directories of the root of the file system which has the symbol "/" . To sum up so far, we opened a console in our home directory root, then we used the command "cd /" which meant change directory to "/" which took us to the root of the file system. Next we typed "ls" the command that lists the contents of the directory you are in, in this case the sub directories immediately below the root of the file system. The file system is a hierarchy starting from the root each sub directory can have further sub directories.

You could of course just click on the "Home" icon on the desktop which opens up a graphical window of your "/root" home directory, then click on the blue up arrow and see all the directories as icons. Slax has all the click, drag, and drop facilities that you are used to but the command line is really easy to use.

So far the directories you have seen are all in computer memory or RAM. They were created when Slax booted up, you can save files in these directories but all that data would be lost if you powered down the computer. Incidentally to power down the computer you can simply type "poweroff" at the command line and press return, alternatively you can click on the blue logo at bottom of the screen and follow the "Log Out" button. To reboot the computer you can type "reboot" at the command line.

In order to keep your work you need to save your files to a non-volatile medium. A hard drive would be an obvious choice but Slax will not write to a NTFS hard drive partition. This is good as you cannot accidentally corrupt your Windows disk. If your hard drive already has a Linux partition you could store your files there. The simple and portable solution is to use a USB flash memory stick. Slax will find a memory stick if you plug one in. Shortly after inserting the memory stick a window will pop up, click OK, your memory stick will now be part of the file system. You will be able to see any directories and files in the graphical window that pops up next.

Close this window as we are going to use the command line. From a console window type at the command line "cd /mnt" this will change directory to the "/mnt" directory which is used to hold the mount points for external file systems. If you now type "ls" you can list the mount points of external file systems on your computer.

root@slax:/mnt# cd /mnt
root@slax:/mnt# ls
hda1/ hda2/ hdd/ live/ sda1/ sda2/ sda3/ sda4/ sdc1/
root@slax:/mnt#

If you have more USB storage devices there will be others for example if you have a USB hard drive with four partitions it could be sda1/, sda2/, sda3/, sda4/, and a memory stick could be sdb1/ or sdc1/.

When navigating around the file system using "cd" you can give the destination as an absolute path. For example "cd /mnt/sdc1" would take you to "sdc1" from anywhere as you have given the instruction starting from the directory system root. You can give a relative path, because we are already in /mnt we can just type "cd sdc1"

To go back up the directory levels you can use the path instruction "../" that takes you up one level relative to where you are. So, if you are in "/mnt/sdc"1 typing "cd ../" would take you back up to "/mnt" .

1.5 File and Directory Handling

A quick way back to your home directory "/root" is to type "cd ~" or even simpler "cd". This will take you back to "/root" from anywhere. Do this now so you can create a few directories and files to manipulate. Fig 1-3 shows the directories to create .

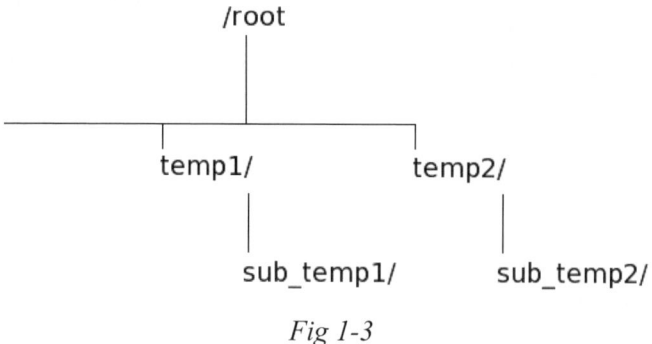

Fig 1-3

To do this use "ls" to see the contents of the directory then "mkdir temp1 temp2", will create the two new directories in "/root".
Then use "ls" to see them as Fig 1-6

```
root@slax:/mnt# cd
root@slax:~# ls
Desktop/
root@slax:~# mkdir temp1 temp2
root@slax:~# ls
Desktop/  temp1/  temp2/
root@slax:~#
```

To create the sub directories you can either navigate into each directory in turn and use "mkdir sub_temp1" in temp1 and "mkdir sub_temp2" in temp2 or you can stay in the "/root" directory and use "mkdir temp1/sub_temp1" and "mkdir temp2/sub_temp2"

Now one of the biggest time savers to try is the auto complete. While in the "/root" directory type "cd t" then press "Tab" this will auto-complete your command up to "ls temp" the point where you have to choose between temp1 and temp 2 add a 1 or a 2 and press return. This will list the contents of that directory.

```
root@slax:~# ls t               <---- type ls t then press "tab"
temp1/ temp2/                   <----gives possible choices
root@slax:~# ls temp            <-----auto completes as far as possible

root@slax:~# ls temp1/          <----"tab" auto completes to here
```

When we come to write programs we will be using the text editor "kate". To start "kate" either hold the "Alt" key down and press "F2", type "kate" in the command box that appears and "return" or click on run. Another alternative is to type "kate" at the console command line. But that uses up a console and clutters the screen as will need to open another console for other operations. Using "kate" is straightforward and needs no explanation. Write a short sentence in "kate" and save the file to one of the directories you created earlier giving it some name say text1.txt. The suffix is not important here. This text editor automatically makes a backup file with same name ending with tilde.

Now at the command line navigate to the directory where you saved the text file and use the command "cp text1.txt /mnt/sda1" (if your memory stick is sda1). This will copy your file to the memory stick.
You can copy from a different directory to the one you are in. Suppose you want to copy a file "text3.txt" from the directory "/mnt/sda1/direc1" to the directory you are currently in, then "cp /mnt/sda1/direc1/text3.txt ./" will do this. The "./" means the current directory.

You can scroll backwards and forwards through previous commands using the up and down arrow keys, also typing history will list and number previous commands

```
100  cd /mnt
101  ls
102  cd
103  mkdir temp1 temp2
104  mkdir temp1/sub_temp1
105  mkdir temp2/sub_temp2
106  ls t
107  ls temp1/
108  history
```

To repeat any of these command say "cd /mnt" you would type "!100".

Most command line commands have options which are invoked by typing the command followed by a space then a dash then the option, for example "ls -l", the long list, will list the files in the directory along with more information about the files. More than one option can be used at once for example "ls -lt" will give the long list with the newest file at the top "ls -ltr" is the same but in the reverse order.

Table 1-1 below gives a list of some useful commands and options. Experiment with these. You can copy files from your hard drive partitions which will be "hda1" "hda2" etc in "/mnt" but you can't write to these partitions if they are MS Windows. You will notice that you can access all the files on your Windows partitions even if under Windows you need a password!

Command	Option	Description
ls		List current directory
	-l	Long list gives more information about files
	-t	Time order
	-S	Size order
	-r	Reverse order
	-a	List all files including hidden files and directories which begin with a dot e.g. .file_name .directory_name/
cd		Change directory, takes a path such as cd /a_directory/a_sub_directory/ or relative path cd ../../another_directory up two levels then down to another_directory
mv		Moves a file to another directory mv file1 /a_directory/a_sub_directory/ or can be used to rename a file mv file_name1 file_name2
cp		Copies a file from one place to another
	-r	Recursive copy will copy a directory and its contents including sub directories
rm		Removes a file i.e. deletes it
	-r	When applied to a directory removes the directory and all of its contents and sub directories- **Dangerous!**
rmdir		Removes a directory providing it is empty
less		Prints the contents of a file to the screen use q to escape. While in "less" "/a word" will search for "a word" Type q to exit.
cat		Prints file contents to the command line.
df		List details of drives
	-h	Outputs sizes in human readable form
lsusb		List USB devices with information

Table 1-1

1.6 Wild Cards

Wild cards allow you to select multiple files, which share a common part to their names or even select all the files in a directory. The two wild cards are "*" and "?".
To delete all the files in a directory use "rm *". Suppose there are four files in a directory as here. I have written them like this to make it easier to follow the logic.

app10serial

app10serial_old

app1serial

app1serial_old

Using "rm app*" would remove all files beginning with "app".
The "*" means any number of undefined characters after "app"

Using "rm *serial" would remove all files ending in "serial" not app10serial_old and app1serial_old.
This is because "serial" has been defined after "*" not "serial_old"

Using "rm app?serial*" would remove all files except "app10serial and "app10serial_old".
The "?" means one undefined character

1.7 Redirection

If you want to create a file with the out put of a command you type the command followed by ">" and then invent a file name. For example.

root@slax:~# ls > dir_list.txt
root@slax:~#

root@slax:~# cat dir_list.txt

Which will print the new file to the screen, giving something like this.

18

Desktop/
dir_list.txt
temp1/
temp2/

1.8 Working With The Python Programs

Throughout the book you will be presented with Python programs, these do not have to be typed out by you as they are all on the Slax CD in the "/root/book/programs/" directory. Each chapter's programs are in a separate subdirectory. I would strongly recommend copying all the program directories to a USB memory stick and working from the directory on the stick, any changes that you make will not get lost. Suppose your memory stick is "sda1" the instruction for copying all the directories recursively is as follows.

root@slax:~#cp -r /book/programs /mnt/sda1

You do not need much space for these programs as they are just text files.

1.9 File Permissions

Linux is a multi user system. Normally it is not recommended to operate as root as you have the authority to do all sorts of damage, and mistakes can be made. However this is not really a problem with a live operating system that is on a CD. You can of course delete data from a memory stick, but if you delete something from the operating system a reboot will fix it. Because Linux is designed to allow different users each file has a set of permissions that allow the users permission to read from, write to, or execute files. To see this change directory to "/root/firefox" then use "ls -l" sometimes referred to as long list, this will produce the following. I have only shown the first few lines.

```
root@slax:~/firefox# ls -l
total 17744
-rw-r--r-- 1 root root   177 Nov 2 23:01 README.txt
-rw-r--r-- 1 root root   825 Nov 2 23:01 Throbber-small.gif
-rw-r--r-- 1 root root   1233 Dec 28 18:14 active-update.xml
-rw-r--r-- 1 root root   2126 Nov 2 23:01 application.ini
-rw-r--r-- 1 root root   2067 Nov 2 23:01 blocklist.xml
-rw-r--r-- 1 root root   232 Nov 2 23:01 browserconfig.properties
drwxr-xr-x 3 root root   280 Nov 2 23:01 chrome/
```

drwxr-xr-x 2 root root   1481 Dec 8 23:38 components/
-rwxr-xr-x 1 root root   45760 Nov 2 23:01 crashreporter*

. . . .

Each line is a directory or a file. The first character states if it is directory, then there are three groups of three characters, "r", "w", "x" or "-". The first group of three, indicate the permissions given to the owner. The second group of three characters, indicate the permissions given to a group of users and the third group of three characters are the permissions give to the other users. The next two names are the owner and the group. Finally there is the size of the file in bytes and the date and time it was created. The permissions are read write and execute.

The owner of the file can change the permissions by using the command "chmod" followed by a three digit number.

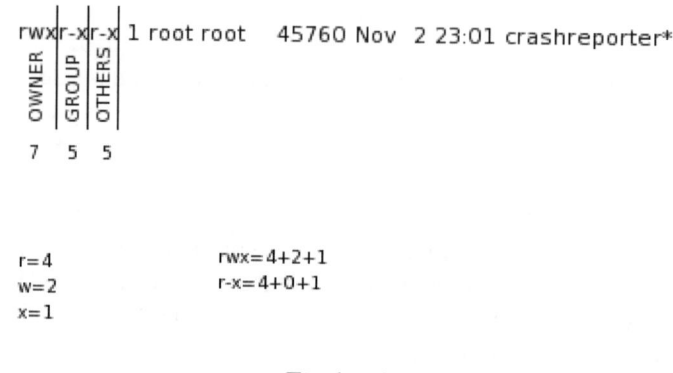

Fig 1 – 4

Fig 1 - 4 shows how the number is derived, to set these file permission you would use "chmod 755 crashreporter"

The meaning of the permissions when applied to a directory are **read**, (means you can read the names and other information about files in that directory), **write**, (means you can delete files create files and copy files to that directory), and **execute** (means you can traverse that directory to reach another.)

Throughout this book the operating system will be used by root.

1.10 BASH Scripts

You can put command line instructions into a text file and make that file executable. This topic will only get a mention here. Prog 1 – 1 below is a very simple script that will create a file in the "/root" directory and write a list of all the files and directories of the directory it is in.


```
#!/usr/bin/bash
ls -la > /root/file_list.txt
```

> *Prog 1 – 1*

If you write a BASH script you have to start with the line "#!/usr/bin/bash" which tells the program loader that this is a script and to use the interpreter "bash". The next line lists all the files and directory names and information and redirects to a file it will create in the "/root" directory. In order to use the script you have to "chmod" it, and to run it type its path and name. Suppose you put it in the "firefox" directory "/root/firefox/prog0101.sh" will run it. If you navigate to the "firefox" directory then "./prog0101.sh" will run it.

The reason I have mentioned this topic is that later in chapter 11 some scripts will need to be amended for the purpose of creating customized live CDs.

1.11 The X Server

The console that you have been using is actually a virtual console and is generated by the X server that handles the graphic displays that are now normal to most computer users. It is possible to use Linux without X and all you get is the command line interface, although you can skip from screen to screen and have several things running at once. Throughout the book we will be using the X server and the CD starts it automatically. The non-X environment is still useful for embedded systems where resources are low. There are text only web browsers like "Lynx" available.

Chapter 2

Getting Started with Python

2.1 Introduction

Microprocessors handle numbers that are represented physically by using the binary system implemented as voltages. When a computer handles text it is still handling numbers by way of the American Standard Code for Information Interchange (ASCII) code. For example the character "A" is 65. At a most basic level a microprocessor could have its code written by a human in machine code, these are the numbers that represent the instructions and data. An improvement is to use an assembler, which is a program that accepts human friendly abbreviations for the machine code and writes a file that is the machine code.

On the left Prog 2-1a is a short program written for the assembler FASM.

```
;prog_02_01.asm

format ELF executable
jmp main
message  db   "It's a lot easier in python!",10
len equ $-message

main:
mov edx, len
mov ecx, message
mov eax, 4
int 0x80


mov eax, 1
int 0x80
```

```
//prog_02_01.c

#include<stdio.h>

int main(){

printf("It's a lot easier in python\n");

return 0;

}
```

Prog 2 - 1a

Prog 2 - 1b

The source code "prog_02_01.asm" has been assembled to an executable file "assembler_demo" and is on the CD.

If you want to, you can run it at the command line as follows, make sure you are in the

22

same directory as the file and then type ./assembler_demo , actually ./a "tab" should then auto-complete for you.

root@slax:~# ./assembler_demo
It's a lot easier in python!
root@slax:~#

Assembler is still used where speed is important or in applications such as microcontrollers. It requires knowledge of the microprocessor's architecture and other hardware details by the programmer.

Prog 2 - 1b does the same as the assembler program, using the higher level language C. C uses a program called a compiler that allows you to write in a form that is more readable and deals with the details of the hardware. The compiler takes the C source code written by a human and compiles it into executable files that can be run by the processor through your operating system.

So if that's what a C compiler does why are we going to need Python? Basically **Python is a whole lot easier to use than C**. Python is an interpreted language. The Python interpreter program has to be installed on the computer for the operating system you are using. Python is a cross platform language. Python takes your script and compiles it into something called byte code that runs on a virtual machine on your operating system, this compilation occurs when you start a program. This is slower than a compiled C program but what is too slow depends on what your doing. Python is certainly fast enough for the applications in this book.

In Python the above programs would be:

print   "It's a lot easier in Python!"

Software can be thought of as being layered. Ultimately we are dealing with electronics or even electro-mechanical devices. The code at the low level that controls the hardware is written in assembler or a compiled language like "C". These languages are said to be 'close to the metal'. C was once considered to be a high level language. It is more convenient and productive to use a higher language like Python that makes use of this lower level code, and at the same time insulates the programmer from all this detail. This is called abstraction. There is a library of code already written to deal with USB, and the interface chips that we are going to use. In order to use this library a set of bindings have been written so that part of this library can be used in Python. These bindings are simple functions that, for example, turn an output on or off. The cost of abstracting away the low level detail is speed of operation, but if it is still fast enough then it will work. The plus side is the speed of writing the program Obviously having fewer lines of code will be quicker to write but also fewer lines of code mean fewer opportunities to make mistakes. The code will be more readable, and easier to modify at a later date. You can concentrate on the overall operation of the system you are making. This abstraction also applies when writing graphic user-interfaces. Writing low level code for graphics and mouse clicks and the like is something that you do not have to do. In Python all this is wrapped up in relatively simple functions.

2.2 Start Programming

Open "kate" the text editor and type in the following program, you can miss out the lines beginning "#".

#prog_02_02.py

```
for n in range (0, 100):
    print  'Hello World'
    print n

print 'End of program'
```

Prog 2 - 2 hello.py

Save the file as "prog_02_02.py" in the "/root" directory.
At the command line type "python hello.py". The .py means it's a Python script. Programs will be run by Python without it but it's the convention and kate will auto-indent and colour and embolden you script to make it more readable.

This four line program introduces some new concepts. The first line creates a variable n and initially assigns it to the integer 0. The next two lines are indented, **this indentation is a key part of Python programs**, in this case we are looping round and round each time n is assigned another integer value and stopping at 99. The indented lines are executed on every loop. Then the program moves on to the last line. The amount of indentation does not matter but it must be consistent, the recommendation is four spaces and don't use tabs. You will find that "kate" on this CD has been set to indent four spaces when you press the tab key. Missing this colon before an indented line will produce a syntax error. Python is

24

also case sensitive.

All of the programs are on the CD in sub-directories of the "/root/book/" directory. I have found that that there are two main reasons for programming errors, the first is not understanding what you are doing, the second is being a bad typist. I would encourage you not only to run the programs as they are, but play with them, improve them and make them do something else. The error messages are useful training aids!

#prog_02_03.py

```
for n in range (0, 100):
    if n != 95 and n != 97:          #The "!=" means check for inequality,
        print 'Hello World'          #this will be dealt with later.
        print n
    else:
        print 'Missed out this value of n'

print 'End of program'
```

Prog 2 - 3

Prog 2 - 3 is based on the first program, but with an added "if" statement that checks to see that n is not equal to 95 and not equal to 97 if this is true the indented lines are executed if not the indented line after else: is executed.

It is useful to put comments in program scripts to help explain how a program works. These comments are prefixed with "#" to tell Python to ignore anything after this on this line.

You have a choice as to how you create your program scripts. My preference is to use a standard text editor in this case "kate" there is however a dedicated application called "idle" which is a text based Python programming environment. It makes no difference which method you use as the code is the same.

2.3 Idle

To open idle type "idle" at the command line or "Alt F2" to get a the command box to enter "idle". You will be presented with a window with the Python interactive prompt, which will be the subject of the next topic. To create a text file use the "File" drop down menu and choose "New Window". If you press "F1" while in idle and you are on line you will be taken to the reference documentation at "http://www.python.org/doc/current/".

2.4 Interactive Sessions

A useful feature of Python is the interactive session where you can enter individual lines of code at the Python prompt without first saving them as a text file. If you type at the command line "python" the following will result.

```
root@slax:~# python
Python 2.6.2 (r262:71600, Sep 29 2009, 15:47:35)
[GCC 4.2.4] on linux2
Type "help", "copyright", "credits" or "license" for more information.
>>>
```

The '>>>' is the Python interactive prompt, try the following.

```
>>> a=12
>>> b=4
>>> c=5
>>> print a/b
3
>>> print a/c
2
>>>
```

Something seems to be wrong here! 12 divided by 4 is 3 but 12 divided by 5 should be 2.4. Nothing actually is wrong here apart from the answer, we will deal with the cause of this apparent error next. To exit from the interactive prompt, type "Ctr d".

2.5 Data Types

2.5.1 Integers

As mentioned previously, microprocessors handle numbers. But these numbers are interpreted in different ways. The different ways of interpreting numbers are what is referred to as data types.

Integers are the set of numbers that include all positive and negative whole numbers including zero {…..............-5, -4, -3, -2, -1, 0, 1, 2, 3, 4, 5,.............. }.

In the previous interactive example a variable "a" was assigned to the object 12 an integer. This object is an area of memory containing the value 12 and marked as being an integer. Also "b" and "c" were assigned to integer objects, when Python carries out the division of two integers it gives the answer as an integer. The answer will be rounded down.

```
>>> 13/11
1
>>> 11/13
0
>>>
```

The % operator when used with two integers returns the remainder of a division.

```
>>> 13%11
2
>>>
```

Floats

Integers are fine for counting things like the number of times to execute instructions in a loop or the number of characters in a sentence but in maths we need to deal with fractional numbers such as the 12/5 above.
The data type that handles fractional numbers is the "float" to tell Python that your number is a "float" you simply express it with a decimal point. Try this.

```
>>> a=12
>>> c=5.0
>>> print a/c
```

2.4
>>>

Here "c" has been assigned to a float object 5.0, but "a" is still an integer, Python carries out floating point arithmetic if one or more of the numbers is a float and returns the answer as a float.

This is an important thing to remember as using integers when the answer should be a float can be a cause of bugs in your programs.

2.5.2 Strings and Writing To and Reading From Files

Humans need text to interact with programs, Python has the string data type. To assign a variable to a string you include your string in either single or double quotation marks, see below:

```
>>> s="A string of characters between double quotation marks"
>>> print s
 A string of characters between double quotation marks
>>>
>>> s='A string of characters between single quotation marks'
>>> print s
 A string of characters between single quotation marks
>>>
```

This option allows you to include " within ' ' or ' within " " .

```
>>> s="This is John's string"
>>> print s
This is John's string
>>>
```

```
>>> s='John said "This is my string".'
>>> print s
John said "This is my string".
>>>
```

You can join strings together this is called concatenation.

```
>>> first_string = 'There are 8 bits '
>> second_string = 'in a byte'
>>> print first_string + second_string
There are 8 bits in a byte
>>>
```

There are a couple of things to note here. The character 8 was treated a text character not a number. The "+" sign was not used as in addition but as the operator to join the strings, this is what is called operator overloading. Due to circumstances where two strings are involved Python knows the meaning of "+".

We don't necessarily have to assign a variable to a string. A string appeared in the first Python program prog_02_02.py
where we used the line "print "Hello World". Here we dealt with the string object directly ;
it is called a string literal.
Try this interactive session.

```
>>> print 'There are 2 bytes '  'in a word.'
There are 2 bytes in a word.
>>>
```

Here we have concatenated two string literals but the "+" is not required. To end an interactive session and return to the normal Linux command prompt type "Ctrl d"
If you have a long string that runs to more than one line you can use triple quotation marks and then the string that gets printed is exactly as you typed it, including new lines.

#prog_02_04.py

```
long_string = '''The best way of typing long strings with lots of
newlines and perhaps
short
lines is to use triple quotation marks. This also allows you to use "double" and
'single' quotation marks in your text.'''
print long_string
```

Prog 2 - 4

Running this program gives the following output.

root@slax:~# python prog_02_05.py
The best way of typing long strings with lots of
newlines and perhaps
short
lines is to use triple quotation marks. This also allows you to use "double" and
'single' quotation marks in your text.
root@slax:~#

Shortly we will deal with reading and writing from files as this will be needed to store data from, say, a data logger. It might be necessary to generate names for files and to do this we need to manipulate strings. Go back to the text editor "kate" and type in the following program and save it as "prog_02_05.py"


```
#prog_02_05.py

s1 = 'File_'
s3 = '.dat'
for n in range (0, 10):
    s2 = str(n)
    print s1 + s2 + s3
```

Prog 2 - 5

Now run it from the command line to get the following.

root@slax:~# python prog_02_05.py
File_0.dat
File_1.dat
File_2.dat
File_3.dat
File_4.dat
File_5.dat
File_6.dat
File_7.dat
File_8.dat
File_9.dat
root@slax:~#

30

Note the line "s = str(n)". This is a built in function in Python that converts an object into a string.
Another way of achieving this is to use the format operator "%" at an interactive session try this.

```
>>> s = 'File_%d.dat' % (99)
>>> print s
File_99.dat
>>>
```

Look at the first line. We have a string with "%d" in the middle, after the string there is a space then the % operator then 99 in brackets. The %d means an integer goes here, the value of this integer is determined by the 99 in brackets following the second %. This is another example of operator overloading.

Here we format a string with a string and a new expression, which raises numbers by a power.

```
>>> print '%s %d' % ('To raise 2 to the power 32 we can use the expression 2**32 to give ',2**32)
To raise 2 to the power 32 we can use the expression 2**32 to give  4294967296
>>>
```

In the brackets we have what is called a "tuple" consisting of, in this case, two objects that are to be used by our formatting. The objects in the tuple must match the requirements of the formatting.

In program 5 we created the names for 10 files. If we repeat this for 20 files by increasing the range of n to 20 we still get our file names but after File_9.dat will come File_10.dat. It might be that we want the files to be listed in a directory consecutively or perhaps opened and read in order by another program. File_10.dat will come before File_2.dat. The way round this program is to add leading zeros.

#prog_02_06.py

```
s1 = 'File_'
s3 = '.dat'
for n in range (0, 20):
```

```
s2 = 'File_%02d' % (n)
print s1 + s2 + s3
```

Prog 2 - 6

In the string formatting line %02d means a leading zero is added to make the printed integer two figures long this gives the output.

```
root@slax:~# python prog_02_06.py
File_00.dat
File_01.dat
File_02.dat
File_03.dat
File_04.dat
File_05.dat
File_06.dat
File_07.dat
File_08.dat
File_09.dat
File_10.dat
File_11.dat
File_12.dat
File_13.dat
File_14.dat
File_15.dat
File_16.dat
File_17.dat
File_18.dat
File_19.dat
root@slax:~#
```

This means these files would be listed in the correct order. But we haven't created any files, just file names so let's put together some of what has been covered and start dealing with reading and writing to files. I have covered file writing and reading here because it provides some interesting exercises for strings.

```
#prog_02_07.py

f = open('File_01.dat', 'w')
f.write('This will be in the file')
f.close()
```

Prog 2 – 7

The first line of the program creates a variable "f" and assigns it to an open file "File_01.dat" which has been opened for writing. Warning, if the file already exists its content will be lost.

Most objects in Python have methods, which carry out some action. An example of a method being called is the second line of the program "f.write(.....)", the "f" is followed by a dot and then the method which in this case is to write to the file. Inside the parenthesis is the argument for the method, or what is to be written to the file. The last line calls another method, to close the file.

If you open "File_01.dat" with kate it will have the line "This will be in the file". Prog 2 - 8 will open the file for appending, if the file does not exist it will create it.

```
#prog_02_08.py

f = open('File_01.dat', 'a')
f.write(' This will be appended to the file.')
f.close
```

Prog 2 - 8

Note if the file is still open in "kate" a message box will flash up, just click on reload.
This time if you look at "File_01.dat" the line will be "This will be in the file This will be appended to the file", note that the two strings will run together so we need to remember to include any necessary spaces between sentences. If you want a newline you have to write the ASCII byte that means newline. This is achieved by writing "\n" to the file. The "\" is the escape character and what happens depends on what character comes immediately after it.

```
#prog_02_09.py

f = open('File_01.dat', 'a')
f.write('\nThis will be appended to the file on a new line.')
f.close
```

Prog 2 - 9

File_01.dat will now contain:

This will be in the file This will be appended to the file.
This will be appended to the file on a new line.

Prog 2 – 10 reads from the file.

#prog_02_10.py

```
f = open('File_01.dat', 'r')
s = f.read()
f.close()
print s
```

Prog 2 - 10

The output of this program prints the content of the file to the command line.

root@slax:~# python prog_02_10.py
This will be in the fileThis will be appended to the file
This will be appended to the file on a new line.

Now to generate the 20 files and write to them.

#prog_02_11.py

```
s1 = 'File_'
s3 = '.dat'
for n in range (0, 20):
    s2 = '%02d' % (n)
    f = open(s1 + s2 + s3, 'w')
```

34

```
s4 = 'Text for File_' + s2 + '.dat'
f.write(s4)
f.close
```

Prog 2 – 11

If you now do a list at the command line depending on what else is in your directory you will get something like this..

```
root@slax:~# ls
Desktop/    File_03.dat File_07.dat File_11.dat File_15.dat File_19.dat
File_00.dat File_04.dat File_08.dat File_12.dat File_16.dat book/
File_01.dat File_05.dat File_09.dat File_13.dat File_17.dat firefox/
File_02.dat File_06.dat File_10.dat File_14.dat File_18.dat prog_02_11.py*
root@slax:~#
```

The created files are there in order. Now to read all the files and print them out.

#prog_02_12.py

```
s1 = 'File_'
s3 = '.dat'
for n in range (0, 20):
    s2 = '%02d' % (n)
    f = open(s1 + s2 + s3, 'r')      # This line is different, it opens to read.
    s4=f.read()                      #This line is different .
    print s4                         # This line is different.
    f.close
```

Prog 2 - 12

The two files don't differ by much, only three lines. Running Prog 2 - 11 gives this output.

root@slax:~# python prog_02_12.py

Text for File_01.dat
Text for File_02.dat
Text for File_03.dat
Text for File_04.dat
Text for File_05.dat
Text for File_06.dat
Text for File_07.dat
Text for File_08.dat
Text for File_09.dat
Text for File_10.dat
Text for File_11.dat
Text for File_12.dat
Text for File_13.dat
Text for File_14.dat
Text for File_15.dat
Text for File_16.dat
Text for File_17.dat
Text for File_18.dat
Text for File_19.dat
root@slax:~#

You might have discovered a few error messages already if you have had typing errors. Some errors will occur as soon as you try to run a program; errors such as incorrect or missing indents, perhaps a missing quotation mark on the end of a string. Sometimes errors don't always show up and the program will perform happily until there is a change of circumstances that you have not allowed for. If you delete the File_03.dat files and run prog_02_12.py again this will happen.

root@slax:~# python prog_02_12.py
Text for File_00.dat
Text for File_01.dat
Text for File_02.dat
Traceback (most recent call last):
  File "prog_02_12.py", line 6, in <module>
    f=open(s1+s2+s3,'r')   # This line is different, it opens to read
IOError: [Errno 2] No such file or directory: 'File_03.dat'
root@slax:~#

36

The program has aborted at line 6 on the fourth loop because "File_03.dat" does not exist. Python tries to help by printing out where things went wrong. There is a weakness in the program in that I have not allowed for the possibility of the files being opened for reading being non-existant..

```
#prog_02_13.py

s1 = 'File_'
s3 = '.dat'
for n in range (0, 20):

    s2 = '%02d' % (n)
    try:                                 #New statement.
        f = open(s1 + s2 + s3, 'r')      #Line that might fail.
        s4=f.read()
        print s4
        f.close
    except:                              #New statement.
        print 'Unable to open' + s1 + s2 + s3
```

Prog 2 – 13

Prog 2 - 13 introduces two new words "try" and "except". Following "try:" the code that might fail is indented. If this code succeeds all is well but if any part of it fails the code indented following "except:" is executed which in this case is a warning printed to the screen. It would not be good enough to just include the file opening line in the try statement because the three following lines would all fail as well if the file could not be opened.

Because the indentation is part of the functionality of the code it forces a certain neatness in layout that makes the code more readable.

Running the program with "File_03.dat missing gives.

```
root@slax:~# python prog_02_13.py
Text for File_00.dat
Text for File_01.dat
Text for File_02.dat
Unable to open File_03.dat
Text for File_04.dat
Text for File_05.dat
Text for File_06.dat
Text for File_07.dat
Text for File_08.dat
Text for File_09.dat
Text for File_10.dat
Text for File_11.dat
Text for File_12.dat
Text for File_13.dat
Text for File_14.dat
Text for File_15.dat
Text for File_16.dat
Text for File_17.dat
Text for File_18.dat
Text for File_19.dat
root@slax:~#
```

Prog 2 – 14 below prints out the ASCII codes from 32 onwards, the earlier ones are control codes. There is a new data type used in this program; the "character", which is a single character string. The string "s" could have been formatted on one line but would not have been as readable, as the line would have wrapped round .
The program increments "n" from 32 to 63. During each pass through the loop it prints one entry in each column.
The first column is for codes 32 to 63, the second 64 to 95. Hence, "n+32" . The third 96 to 127, hence "n+64".

The function str() will take its argument and convert it to a string. An integer such as 65 will be printed as 65; its argument does not need to be a an integer. The function chr() takes as its argument an integer between 0 and 255 and prints the ASCII character for that integer value.

```
#prog_02_14.py

output_file = open('ascii_list.txt', 'w')
for n in range (32, 64):                              #Prints one entry in each column for every loop.
    s =  str(n) +' is ascii for  ' + chr(n) + '\t\t\t'    #Formats first column codes 32 to 63.
    s =  s + str(n + 32) +' is ascii for  ' + chr(n + 32) + '\t\t\t'   #Formats second column codes
                                                      #64 to 95.
    s =  s + str(n + 64) +' is ascii for  ' + chr(n + 64) + '\t\t\t\n'  #Formats third column codes
                                                      #96 to 127.
    output_file.write(s)

output_file.close()
```
Prog 2 - 14

The following is the text from the resulting file "ascii_list.txt".

32 is ascii for	64 is ascii for @	96 is ascii for `
33 is ascii for !	65 is ascii for A	97 is ascii for a
34 is ascii for "	66 is ascii for B	98 is ascii for b
35 is ascii for #	67 is ascii for C	99 is ascii for c
36 is ascii for $	68 is ascii for D	100 is ascii for d
37 is ascii for %	69 is ascii for E	101 is ascii for e
38 is ascii for &	70 is ascii for F	102 is ascii for f
39 is ascii for '	71 is ascii for G	103 is ascii for g
40 is ascii for (	72 is ascii for H	104 is ascii for h
41 is ascii for)	73 is ascii for I	105 is ascii for i
42 is ascii for *	74 is ascii for J	106 is ascii for j
43 is ascii for +	75 is ascii for K	107 is ascii for k
44 is ascii for ,	76 is ascii for L	108 is ascii for l
45 is ascii for -	77 is ascii for M	109 is ascii for m
46 is ascii for .	78 is ascii for N	110 is ascii for n
47 is ascii for /	79 is ascii for O	111 is ascii for o
48 is ascii for 0	80 is ascii for P	112 is ascii for p
49 is ascii for 1	81 is ascii for Q	113 is ascii for q
50 is ascii for 2	82 is ascii for R	114 is ascii for r
51 is ascii for 3	83 is ascii for S	115 is ascii for s
52 is ascii for 4	84 is ascii for T	116 is ascii for t
53 is ascii for 5	85 is ascii for U	117 is ascii for u
54 is ascii for 6	86 is ascii for V	118 is ascii for v
55 is ascii for 7	87 is ascii for W	119 is ascii for w
56 is ascii for 8	88 is ascii for X	120 is ascii for x
57 is ascii for 9	89 is ascii for Y	121 is ascii for y
58 is ascii for :	90 is ascii for Z	122 is ascii for z
59 is ascii for ;	91 is ascii for [	123 is ascii for {

60 is ascii for <	92 is ascii for \	124 is ascii for |
61 is ascii for =	93 is ascii for]	125 is ascii for }
62 is ascii for >	94 is ascii for ^	126 is ascii for ~
63 is ascii for ?	95 is ascii for _	127 is ascii for

As well as joining strings we can slice strings. Try this.

```
>>> s='abcdefghijklmnopqrstuvwxyz'
>>> print s[15] + s[24]  + s[19] +s[7] + s[14] + s[13]
python
>>>
```

Here we have created a string that is the alphabet and then sliced individual characters from the string. Remember that numbering starts from 0. The letter z here is number 25.

To make things clear for the next few exercises we will use the string "01234567899876543210" which is not a number but a string of characters that conveniently enumerates their positions. **Remember counting starts from 0**.

```
>>> s='01234567899876543210'
```

```
>>> print s[2:6]
2345
```
    #When the first index is positive the first character of the
    #slice is from that position.
    #When the second index is positive the last character is the
    #one before that position.

```
>>> print s[-6:-2]
5432
```
    #When the first index is negative the first character of the
    #slice is the one after that position counting from the right.
    #When the second index is negative the last character of
    #the slice is from that position counting from the right.
```
>>>
```
    #This is logical as it is mirror image.

```
>>> print s[2:-2]
2345678998765432
>>>
```

```
>>> print s[2:]          #If one of the indices is missing the slice continues to the end of
```
the string.
234567899876543210
>>>

```
>>> print s[:-2]
```
012345678998765432
>>>

One important point is that strings are immutable, that is they can't be changed in place.

```
>>> string1 = 'abcd'
>>> string1[0] = 'b'
```
Traceback (most recent call last):
  File "<stdin>", line 1, in <module>
TypeError: "str" object does not support item assignment
>>>

Here I have tried to change the first character in place and it is not allowed. I can however slice the string and it becomes a new object. Then assign the variable 'string1' to the new object, followed by concatenating another string to it.

```
>>> string1 = string1[1:]
>>> string1
```
"bcd"
```
>>> string1 = 'b' + string1
>>> string1
```
'bbcd'
>>>

A common requirement is to find a sub-string in a string. Strings have a method that does that. The method ".find()" returns the position of the first occurrence of that sub-string.

```
>>> the_string = 'Python is a really good language.'
>>> the_sub_string = 'good'
>>> position = the_string.find(the_sub_string)
>>> print position
```
19
```
>>> print the_string[19:]
```
good language.

>>>

2.5.3 Lists

Lists are objects that are lists of objects. They provide a means of handling data, each member of a list is indexed by its position in the list. Like strings they can be concatenated and sliced. A list is contained between "[]" brackets and members of the list are separated by commas. The following shows this.

```
>>> l1=[0, 1, 2, 3, 'four', 'five']
>>> l1
[0, 1, 2, 3, 'four', 'five']
>>> l2=[6.0, 7.0, ['a list within', 'a list']]
>>> l2
[6.0, 7.0, ['a list within', 'a list']]
>>> l3 = l1 + l2
>>> l3
[0, 1, 2, 3, 'four', 'five', 6.0, 7.0, ['a list within', 'a list']]
>>> l3[4:]
['four', 'five', 6.0, 7.0, ['a list within', 'a list']]
```

Objects that are members of a list within a list are indexed like this

```
>>> l3[8][1]
'a list'
>>>
```

The first index after l3[8] is item eight, the list within the list and the second index [1] is item one, "a list".

Lists are mutable; meaning you can change them in place.

```
>>> l4=[0,1,2,3,4,5]
>>> l4[2]='changed in place'
>>> l4
[0, 1, 'changed in place', 3, 4, 5]
>>>
```

Lists can grow and shrink. You can append a single object to the end of a list with the ".append()" method.

```
>>> l4=[0, 1, 2, 3, 4, 5]
>>> l4.append('six')
>>> l4
[0, 1, 2, 3, 4, 5, 'six']
>>>
```

When you concatenate a list a new list is created and you either assign a new variable or re-use a variable. If you try and re-assign the list variable with append() you will lose the reference to the list, see here.

```
>>> l5=['q','w','e','r','t']
>>> l5=l5.append('y')
>>> l5
>>>                              #Gone!
```

l5 does not get re-assigned to the list but a value of "None" is returned by the method. Append() changes the list in place so the variable is still assigned to it. Like this.

```
>>> l5=['q','w','e','r','t']
>>> l5.append('y')
>>> l5
['q', 'w', 'e', 'r', 't', 'y']
```

You can delete items with the "del" statement

```
>>> l5
['q', 'w', 'e', 'r', 't', 'y']
>>> del l5[1:3]
>>> l5
['q', 'r', 't', 'y']
>>>
```

You can use the .pop() method to pop the last item off the end.

```
>>> l5
```

['q', 'r', 't', 'y']
>>> p = l5.pop()
>>> l5
['q', 'r', 't']
>>> p
'y'
>>>

You can put a list in order with the ".sort()" method

l6=[7, 5, 3, 'F', 'A', 'f', 'a', ['z', 'y', 'x']]
>>> l6.sort()
>>> l6
[3, 5, 7, ['z', 'y', 'x'], 'A', 'F', 'a', 'f']

Note that the included list ['z', 'y', 'x'] has not been sorted, that's because it was not asked to be. To sort this nested list you would use.

l6=[7,5,3,'F','A','f','a',['z','y','x']]
>>> l6[-1].sort()
>>> l6
[7, 5, 3, 'F', 'A', 'f', 'a', ['x', 'y', 'z']]

A trap you will fall into sooner or later is trying to access a member of a list that's not there. This will raise an error.

>>> l7=[0, 1, 2, 3, 4, 5, 6, 7]
>>> l7[8]
Traceback (most recent call last):
  File "<stdin>", line 1, in <module>
IndexError: list index out of range
>>>

This is another one of those errors that might not come to light straight away but might depend on the circumstances of your program use.

As well as finding sub strings as we did before it can be useful to split a string at certain characters
Consider the next program that will read a file 'sample1.txt' and output the variable as a list.

There are 8 bits in a byte
2 bytes are a word
4 bytes are a double word

sample1.txt

```
#prog_02_15.py

file = open('sample1.txt')
string = file.read()
string_split = string.split('\n')          #Splits at newlines '\n'.
print string_split

print

string_split = string.split('byte')        #Splits  at the word 'byte'.
print string_split
```

Prog 2 - 15

Running Prog 2 -15 shows how first the text file which is just a string is split into members of a list using the newline as an argument, next the same file is split at the newline at the word "byte".

```
root@slax:~# python prog_02_14.py
['There are 8 bits in a byte', '2 bytes are a word', '4 bytes are a double word']

['There are 8 bits in a ', '\n2 ', 's are a word\n4 ', 's are a double word']
root@slax:~
```

If the file is a comma separated variable file (CSV), which is a type that can be read by spreadsheets, the split function can be used to extract values, as shown by Prog 2 -16. First a CSV file.

1.02, 3.14159, 100, 42, 99, 0.868

sample1.csv

```
#prog_02_16.py

file = open('sample1.csv')
file = file.read()
file_split = file.split(',')                #Splits at commas ',' .
print file_split

for n in  file_split:
   print float(n)
```

Prog 2 - 16

```
root@slax:~# python prog_02_16.py
['1.02', ' 3.14159', ' 100', ' 42', ' 99', ' 0.868']
1.02
3.14159
100.0
42.0
99.0
0.868
root@slax:~#
```

2.5.4 Dictionaries

Dictionaries provide another way of handling objects. They are like lists but instead of indexing them by position they are indexed by a key. The dictionary is enclosed in "{}" and the members are made up of a key and an object like so.

```
>>> d1={'item1': 'a string', 'item2': 99, 'what ever': [1, 2, 3]}
>>> d1
{'item2': 99, 'item1': 'a string', 'what ever': [1, 2, 3]}
```

Here the keys are strings and separated from their objects by colons, the members of the dictionary are separated by commas. Notice that Python does not keep the order of the dictionary. Because position is meaningless with dictionaries there is no concatenation and no slicing. Python changes the order to speed up access.

Members are accessed by a key.

```
>>> d1['what ever']
[1, 2, 3]
```

To add a member you invent a new key like this

```
>>> d1[5]='new'
>>> d1
{'item2': 99, 'item1': 'a string', 5: 'new', 'what ever': [1, 2, 3]}
>>>
```

Keys do not have to be strings. Here, the integer 5 is used as a key. Any immutable object can be used.

To find out what the keys of a dictionary are use ".keys()" method

```
>>> d1.keys()
['item2', 'item1', 5]
>>>
```

To find out the values use the ".values()" method

```
>>> d1.values()
[99, 'a string', 'new']
```

Dictionaries are mutable and can be changed in place.

```
>>> d1
{'item2': 99, 'item1': 'a string', 5: 'new'}
>>> d1['item2'] = 101
>>> d1
{'item2': 101, 'item1': 'a string', 5: 'new'}
>>>
```

2.5.5 Tuples

Tuples are like lists in that they are indexed by position but they are immutable; they can not be changed in place, and they have no methods. They can be concatenated, sliced, and nested. A tuple is enclosed in "()" and separated by commas.

```
>>> t1=(0,1,2,3,'a string')
>>> t1[2]
2
>>>
```

If you want to change an item in place, you can convert the tuple to a list perform the change and then convert back again as shown below.

```
>>> l1 = list(t1)
>>> l1
[0, 1, 2, 3, 'a string']
>>> l1[0] = 'new'
>>> l1
['new', 1, 2, 3, 'a string']
>>> t1=tuple(l1)
>>> l1
['new', 1, 2, 3, 'a string']
>>> t1
('new', 1, 2, 3, 'a string')
>>>
```

2.6 Functions

Functions offer a way of re-using code where the same thing needs to be performed more than once in a program. They also give you a logical way of attacking complicated tasks by breaking them down to smaller tasks.

Program 2 – 15 shows a simple function to add up all the integers between 0 and n, where n is a positive integer. Function definitions start with the word "def" then the name of the function with parenthesis to contain arguments for the function to work on. Note that the first line ends with a colon so the rest of the function is indented. The last line returns an object. After the function is a call to total(), with the argument 10000000. The function returns the integer, "s" is then assigned to this returned integer.

```
#prog_02_17.py

def total(n):
    t = (1 + n) * n/2
    return t

s = total(10000000)
print s
```

Prog 2 -17

Running this gives the answer 50000005000000.

```
root@slax:~# python prog_02_17.py
50000005000000
root@slax:~#
```

If you are wondering where t=(1 + n) * n/2 come from, consider if n was say 5, the sum would be 15 and could be arrived at by writing out the numbers twice like so.

$$(1 + 2 + 3 + 4 + 5$$
$$+ 5 + 4 + 3 + 2 + 1) = 6 + 6 + 6 + 6 + 6 = 6 * 5 = 30$$

The function in Prog 2 - 18 does the same but in a crude number crunching way that involves 10 million loops. If you have a slow computer this could take a little while.

49

```
#prog_02_18.py
def total(n):
    t = 0
    for x in range (0, n + 1):
        t = t + x
    return t
s = total(10000000)
print s
```

Prog 2 -18

In the next program the variable "c" is assigned to a string. Then when the function is called a variable "c" gets assigned to an integer. The last line prints out the string that "c" was assigned to. What is going on here is that we have two entirely different variables both called "c". The reason they are separate is that the variable "c" in the function is only recognized in the function, that is its scope. The "c" that was assigned at the start of the program is a global variable.

```
#prog_02_19.py

c = "This won't affect c in the function"

def pythagoras(a,b):
    c = (a * a + b * b)
    h=pow(c ,0.5)                   #Takes the square root.
    return h

hyp = pythagoras(3 , 4)
print hyp
print c
```

Prog 2 -19

This gives this output.

```
root@slax:~# python prog_02_19.py
5.0
This won't affect c in the function
root@slax:~#
```

2.7 Imports

Imports are a means of bringing more ready-written code into your programs. By importing modules you can access a huge amount of available code. There are modules for advanced maths; accessing the Internet; interfacing with serial ports; one module that will be the subject of chapter 4 for writing graphic user interfaces (GUIs); and another module for dealing with time and many more.

At the Python interactive prompt type "import time", then type time.time() as shown below.

```
>>> import time
>>> time.time()
1255530149.428267
>>>
```

The first line imports the time module and makes available time's namespace meaning all time's attributes. The function time() is a function of module time. To call a function of an imported module you type the module name and a dot and then the function. This function returns the number of seconds since midnight on the 1st of January 1970 (UTC)

This program uses the time.asctime() to print out the time as a string, time.sleep(1) pauses for one second. To stop this program type "Ctrl c".

```
#prog_02_20.py

import time

while 1:          #This means while 1 is true, and it always is, we will deal with later in the chapter.
    print time.asctime()
    time.sleep(1)
```

Prog 2 -20

Prog 2 -21 below is an example of making a very simple moving graphic display from a text interface to plot a sine wave. The "math" and the "time" modules are imported. Comments on the program explain the purpose of the lines. The plotting of the graph is achieved by printing spaces to offset the position of the curve at any time. Every cycle a time stamp is printed. Note in the "range(0, 346, 15)" this steps through the range at

51

intervals of 15, The next step after 345 is 360 which is 0 on the next outer loop. The math function "sin()" requires its argument to expressed in radians, the math module has two conversion functions available to do angle conversions, "degrees()" and "radians()".

```
#prog_02_21.py

import math
import time
start=time.time()                              #Time when program starts.
while 1:                                       #Continuous loop.
    time_stamp = '%.2f seconds' % (time.time()-start)   #Time since start, formatted to 2
                                               #decimal places.

    for d in range (0 , 345, 15):     #Range fom 0 345 for every 15 degrees (360 is 0  again).
        r=math.radians(d)
        a=40*math.sin(r)              #Calculate the amplitude, units are spaces.
        a=int(a)                      #Converts amplitude to an integer.
        if d ==0:
            print time_stamp          #Insert time stamp every cycle '==' is used to check for equality.
        else:                         #This will be dealt with later.
            print '|' + ' '*39 + '|' + ' '*39 + '|'    #Prints  axis and max and min ordinates.
        print ' '*(a + 40) + ""       #Plots curve.
        time.sleep(0.083)             #Sets plotting speed to 0.5 Hz approx
                                      #doesn't allow for the execution time of the program.
```

Prog 2 -21

root@slax:~# python prog_02_21.py
0.0   seconds

2.02 seconds

Fig 2 – 1

53

2.8 Logic

Now for a little bit of logic. Python has a Boolean data type which has two values; one is "True", the other is "False". There are logic operators "and", "or" and "not".

```
>>> False and False
False
>>> False and True
False
>>> True and False
False
>>> True and True
True
>>>
```

To create continuous loops in our programs we have used the expression "while 1:" anything other than 0 is true.

So we can repeat the above with 1s and 0s.

```
>>> 0 and 0
0
>>> 0 and 1
0
>>> 1 and 0
0
>>> 1 and 1
1
>>> 1 and True
True
>>>
```

The logic operators are best explained with truth tables

and		Result
0	0	0
0	1	0
1	0	0
1	1	1

or		Result
0	0	0
0	1	1
1	0	1
1	1	1

not	Result
0	1
1	0

Table 2 - 1

2.9 Bits and Bytes

It is probable that most people reading this book are familiar with the binary system. One of the advantages of high level languages like Python is you do not need to worry about this low level stuff. But that does depend on the application you are writing and as this book is about hardware interfacing there is no getting away from it completely.

A bit is the basic unit of information storage. The word bit is a contraction of the words binary digit. Physically a bit can be anything that can have two states, for example an electrical potential of 5 volts or 0 volts, +12 volts or -12 volts. It can be represented by the values 0 or 1. One bit on its own is not very useful; only having two states. Suppose we have two bits next to each other, the number of possible states now increases to four.

0 0 state 0
0 1 state 1
1 0 state 2
1 1 state 3

In the decimal system there are ten states that a single digit can have, the first state is 0, so when the tenth state is reached, that is the number 9, the next state is 10, one lot of ten and no lots of one. The number 123 means 3 lots of one, 2 lots of ten and 1 lot of a hundred. The binary system is the same the first state is 0 the second state is 1 the next state is 10, no lots of 1 and one lot of 2.

With eight bits next to each other there are 256 possible states 0 to 255. Each extra digit doubles the number of states. A byte is generally taken to be eight bits.

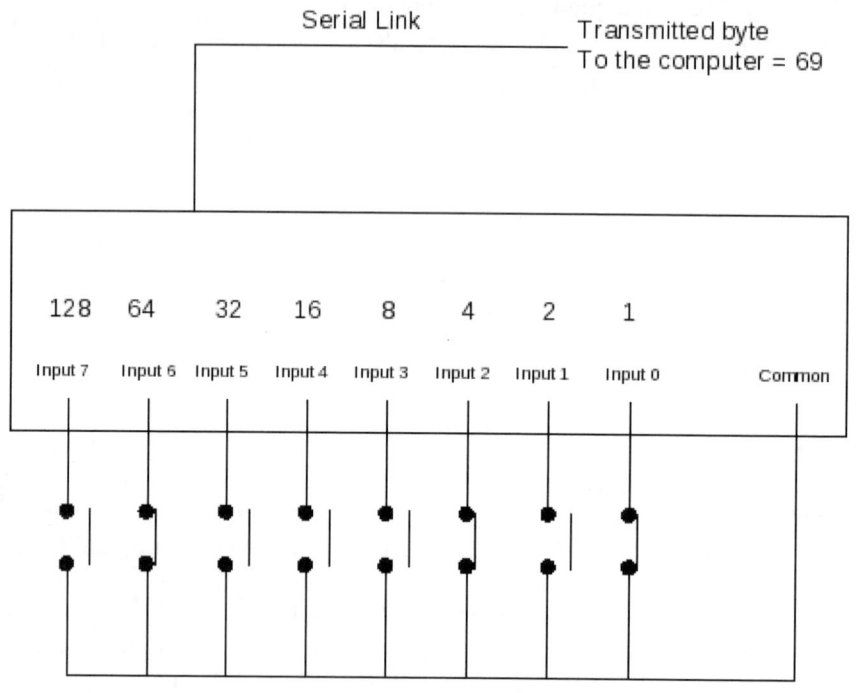

Fig 2 -2

Fig 2 – 2 shows a simplified circuit of what we are aiming for. The device has 8 input/outputs. Here it shown as all inputs. Depending on which switches are closed a certain value of byte will be transmitted to the computer. Any value from 0 to 255 uniquely defines the switch positions, Inputs 0, 2, and 6 are made giving 69. The device can also be configured as outputs or a mixture of inputs and outputs.   Outputs can be written to by sending a byte to the device.

There are bitwise operators in Python that allow us to shift bits left or right. Take the integer 7 which in binary is 111. If the bits are shifted one place to the left the binary number becomes 1110 which is one lot of 8, one lot of 4, and one lot of 2 or 14 in decimal. Moving bits one place to the left multiplies by two and moving to the right divides by two for each place. The shift operator is >> in Python,

56

```
>>> 7 << 1     #One place to the left
14
>>> 7 >> 1     #One place to the right
3
>>>
```

Notice that moving 7 decimal which is 111 binary to the right results in 3 decimal which is 11 binary. The right hand bit has been shifted off the end and is lost.

There are bitwise logic operators, the "&" operator is "bitwise and", and the "|" is the bitwise "or". The integer 14 is 1110 in binary and the integer 11 is 1011 in binary, if we carry out a bitwise "and" operation between the corresponding bits in the two integers we have:

$$
\begin{array}{rl}
1110 & = 14 \text{ decimal} \\
\&\underline{1011} & = 11 \text{ decimal} \\
1010 & = 10 \text{ decimal}
\end{array}
$$

```
>>> 14 & 11
10
>>>
```

There is also an exclusive or operator "^".

$$
\begin{array}{rl}
1110 & = 14 \text{ decimal} \\
\wedge\underline{1011} & = 11 \text{ decimal} \\
0101 & = 5 \text{ decimal}
\end{array}
$$

```
>>> 14 ^ 11
5
>>>
```

Table 2 – 2 shows how the "or" function differs from the "exclusive or" function.

or		Result
0	0	0
0	1	1
1	0	1
1	1	1

^		Result
0	0	0
0	1	1
1	0	1
1	1	0

Table 2 – 2

2.10 Comparison Operators

In programs it is often necessary for the program to take a decision based on the comparison of variables.
We have already used this, for example in Prog 2 – 3 the "!=" was used to test for inequality.
The outcome of the test will determine the action of the program. The comparison operators are summarized in the Table 2 – 3

a == b	True if a is equal to b.
a != b	True if a is not equal to b.
a > b	True if a is greater than b.
a < b	True if a is less than b.
a >= b	True if a is greater than b or if a is equal to b.
a <= b	True if a is less than b or if a is equal to b.

Table 2 – 3

58

The decision based on the comparisons can be made with statements such as "if", "else", "while".

Prog 2 – 22 shows a simple "if" "else" routine.

```
#prog_02_22.py

print 'Input 1 '
s = raw_input()              #raw_inputs() waits for 'return' to be pressed to
                             #assign 's' to the output of the keyboard
                             #buffer.
if s == '1':
    print 'I'

else:
    print "Input was not 1"
```

Prog 2 – 22

Python will not allow you to write "if a=b:" as a test as this is incorrect. When a single "equals" sign is used this is interpreted as an assignment, not a test. A comparison for equality uses two equal signs.

Prog 2 – 22 printed "I" if the input was "1" and "Input was not 1" if the input was not. You only need the "else" statement if you want something else to happen if the test is untrue. Look at program 2 – 23.

```
#prog_02_23.py
print 'Input 1 or 2 or 3 or 4 or  5'
s = raw_input()

if s == '1':
    print 'I'
elif s == '2':
    print 'II'
elif s == '3':
    print 'III'
elif s == '4':
    print 'IV'
elif s == '5':
```

```
    print 'V'
else:
    print 'Input was not 1 or 2 or 3 or 4 or  5'
```

Prog 2 – 23

If the first test is untrue further tests are tried using "elif" and then if all fail the "else" statement.

Comparisons can be used to make a loop conditional Prog 2 – 24 is a simple example.

```
#prog_02_24.py

n = 0
while n < 40:
    print str(n) + ' is less than 40'
    n = n + 1

print str(n) + ' is equal to 40'
```

Prog 2 – 24

2.11 Hexadecimal Notation

Take for example 10111111, which is 191 in decimal. The binary notation is fine if you want to explicitly see which pins are high or low, but it is not a convenient notation for humans to remember numbers in. The problem with using the decimal notation is that it is not convenient to see the binary equivalent. The answer is a notation that uses the base 16, the hexadecimal system. In the decimal system we have 10 digits, so in the hexadecimal system we use 0 to 9 and "a" to "f" to give sixteen digits; "a" is 10 decimal, and "f" is 15 decimal. What makes this so convenient is 15 decimal becomes 1111 binary. Four bits are referred to as a nibble. We can now represent an 8 bit byte with two hexadecimal digits one for the low order nibble and one for the high order nibble.

Binary	Hexadecimal	Decimal
0000 0000	00	0
0000 0001	01	1
0000 1001	09	9
0000 1010	0a	10
0000 1011	0b	11
0000 1100	0c	12
0000 1101	0d	13
0000 1110	0e	14
0000 1111	0f	15
0001 0000	10	16
1010 0000	a0	160
1111 1011	fa	250
1111 1111	ff	255

2.12 Persistence of Objects

When a program ends all data is lost, which might be inconvenient for a control system where user settings would have to be re-entered. Python has a module called "pickle" which can save objects to a file and can recover them next time or by a different program. Prog 2 – 25 is a simple example.

```
#prog_02_25.py
import pickle

try:                            #The file won't exist the first time the program runs
    file=open('store.dat','r')
    data_in=pickle.load(file)   #Unpickles the objects in the file
    file.close()
except:
    data_in=[0,0,0,['']]        #Sets initial values for first time run

print data_in
data_out=[1,2,3,'Persistance']  #Sets values - could be set by the user in a control system
file=open('store.dat','w')
```

61

```
pickle.dump(data_out,file)          #Pickles the data for future use.
file.close()
```

Prog 2 – 25

Running the program the first time or any time the "store.dat" file is missing gives this.

```
root@slax:~# python prog_02_25.py
[0, 0, 0, [''']]
```

Subsequent times the program gives this.

```
root@slax:~# python prog_02_25.py
[1, 2, 3, 'Persistance']
root@slax:~#
```

Compiled Python Files

You might notice files appearing in directories where you have Python scripts with the same name as an existing script but with the extension ".pyc". These are files that the interpreter has created when it decided that the program has not changed and it will be faster to use the compiled byte code it created last time the program ran.

Chapter 3

Object Oriented Programming

3.1 Introduction

So far our programs have been what are called procedural programs. Object orientation is a different way of writing programs. It is about creating software models of real world items as separate objects. These objects contain the data and the functions that are associated with objects. Please be aware that the treatment of this topic is just enough to achieve the aim of producing working interfaces.

We will introduce new concepts known as 'class', and 'inheritance'. The objects we are talking about here are individual instances of a class. You are an instance of the class human. You have a name that can be used to distinguish you from other instances of the class human. The class of human has the attribute height if your name is jsmith your height might be "jsmith.height=1.6

3.2 Class

The block of code that is the class is like a factory that produces instances of that class. These instances encapsulate data and methods, methods being the term used for functions in classes. This is a convenient way of programming, as programs get more complicated.

Let us consider for an initial example the electronic circuit known as a voltage comparator. If the input voltage is above a certain level, which we will call the setpoint, then the output is **on**, otherwise it is **off**.

In Python we could create a class to represent voltage comparators like these, as in Prog 3 - 1a. This program has a class named "Comparator". The class is used to create two instances of voltage comparators that have different setpoints.

To create a class we start with the word "class" then give it a name, in this case "Comparator". It is convention to start class names with a capital letter.

Indented below this first line is the rest of the class. Our class here has two methods.

Moving down to the line "comp1=....", after the end of the class code, this line creates an instance of a voltage comparator I have called "comp1".

 # prog_03_01a.py

```
class Comparator:
    def __init__(self, setpoint):        #Method runs whenever a new instance is created.
        self.switch_level = setpoint
        self.output = False

    def switching(self, voltage):
        self.input_voltage = voltage

        if self.input_voltage > self.switch_level:
            self.output = True
        else:
            self.output = False

#end of class code


comp1 = Comparator(5)                #Creates instance comp1, calls method __init__
comp2 = Comparator(6)                #Creates instance comp2, calls method __init__

print 'comp1 output is ' + str(comp1.output)
print 'comp2 output is ' + str(comp2.output)
```

Prog 3 – 1a

When creating an instance of a class the method "__init__" of that class is called automatically, if it exists. The word "init" has two underscores both sides. Now looking at this method you will see there are two arguments, the first is "self" this means that the function belongs to this instance

The second argument which I have named "voltage" is the argument passed to the "__init__" method whenever a new instance is created, here the value is 5. The next line sets the variable "self.on_level" to 5 which will be the setpoint for the comparator comp1. Again the self means that this variable belongs to the instance being created. The last line of "__init__" sets the variable "self.output" to off or "False".

Moving on to the line "comp2=.......", this line creates another instance of Comparator but

64

this time when "__init__" runs, the setpoint is set to the value 6.

Fig 3 -1 is a pictorial overview of this instance creation.

Looking at the last two lines of the program, these lines print out the states of the outputs. The function switching(self,voltage) has not been called yet.

Running Prog 3 -1a gives the following.

```
root@slax:~# python prog_03_01a.py
comp1 output is False
comp2 output is False
root@slax:~#
```

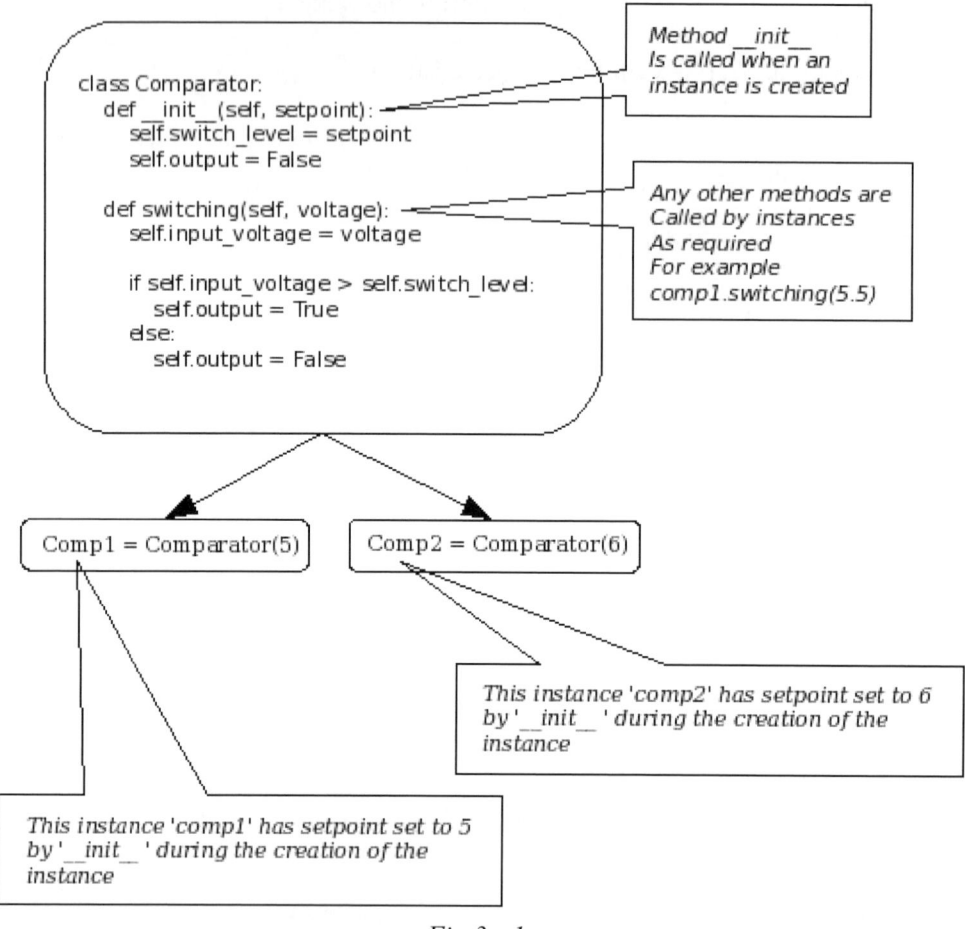

class Comparator:
    def __init__(self, setpoint):
        self.switch_level = setpoint
        self.output = False

    def switching(self, voltage):
        self.input_voltage = voltage

        if self.input_voltage > self.switch_level:
            self.output = True
        else:
            self.output = False

Method __init__
Is called when an
instance is created

Any other methods are
Called by instances
As required
For example
comp1.switching(5.5)

Comp1 = Comparator(5)   Comp2 = Comparator(6)

This instance 'comp2' has setpoint set to 6
by '__init__' during the creation of the
instance

This instance 'comp1' has setpoint set to 5
by '__init__' during the creation of the
instance

Fig 3 - 1

Now let us apply an input voltage of 5.5 to our two instances of the Comparator class.
This is the purpose of the "switching(self, voltage)" method.

To call the "switching()" method of comp1 with an input value of 5.5 you use
"comp1.switching(5.5)" and for comp2, "comp2.switching(5.5)".

Prog 3 - 1b shows the program these lines added and two lines to print out the new output
states.

 # prog_03_01b.py

```
class Comparator:
    def __init__(self, setpoint):        #Method runs whenever a new instance is created
        self.switch_level = setpoint
        self.output = False

    def switching(self, voltage):
        self.input_voltage = voltage

        if self.input_voltage > self.switch_level:
            self.output = True
        else:
            self.output = False

#end of class code

comp1 = Comparator(5)              #Creates instance comp1, calls method __init__
comp2 = Comparator(6)              #Creates instance comp2, calls method __init__

print 'comp1 output is ' + str(comp1.output)
print 'comp2 output is ' + str(comp2.output)

comp1.switching(5.5)
comp2.switching(5.5)

print 'comp1 output is ' + str(comp1.output)
print 'comp2 output is ' + str(comp2.output)
```

Prog 3 - 1b

Running this program produces the following result.

```
root@slax:~# python prog_03_01b.py
comp1 output is False
comp2 output is False
comp1 output is True
comp2 output is False
root@slax:~#
```

Both comparators have the same input voltage, 5.5, but they were created with different setpoints, therefore comp1 switched on and comp2 did not.

3.3 Inheritance

A Schmitt trigger is similar to a voltage comparator but has the property that the switch off voltage is lower than the switch on voltage. The difference between the two switching points is called hysteresis. To write code that acts like a Schmitt trigger we can make use of the Comparator class that has been written. We do this by creating a new class that will be named "SchmittTrigger". The first line of the new class will be "class SchmittTrigger(Comparator)", by putting "Comparator" in parenthesis SchmittTrigger inherits all the variables and methods of class Comparator. When a class name contains more than one word, each word starts with a capital letter.

However any program that is going to use the new SchmittTrigger class must be able to import the namespace of Comparator. Create a file with just the class code block for class Comparator and save it as "comparator.py". Note that when importing a file if you use "import file_name" then to call its methods you have to use "file_name.method()". However, you can use "from file_name import *" which imports all of the namespace and you can use the methods directly by just calling their names. The imported file name does not have the ".py" extension included in the import statement.

```
from comparator import *          #Comparator.py must be in the current directory
                                  #or /usr/local/lib/python2.6 this must contain class Comparator.

class SchmittTriger(Comparator):
    def __init__(self, setpoint, hysteresis):
        Comparator.__init__(self, setpoint)    #This is needed because the inherited __init__ has been
                                               #superceded by the preceding line.
        self.hyst= hysteresis


    def trigger(self, voltage):
        self.input_voltage = voltage
        if self.output == True:
            self.input_voltage = self.input_voltage + self.hyst
        self.switching(self.input_voltage)        #inherited from Comparator

#end of class code

trig1=SchmittTriger(6, 2)                    # On at 6 & off at 4.

for v in (4.0,  4.5, 5.0, 5.5, 6.0, 6.5, 7.0, 6.5, 6.0, 5.5, 5.0, 4.5, 4.0):
    trig1.trigger(v)
    print 'Input voltage = ' + str(v) + '-----Output = ' + str(trig1.output)
```

Prog 3 – 2

Looking first at the "__init__" method for class "SchmittTrigger" we have to pass two arguments when creating an instance; one being the setpoint as before and the other is the hysteresis value.

If you are writing a class that inherits from another and you do not have a "__init__" method in the new class the "__init__" method of the parent class will be run. However, here we have written a new "__init__" method which supersedes the one in class Comparator. That is why the next line of code calls "Comparator.__init__(self, setpoint)" to run.

After the class code, an instance "trig1" is created with a setpoint of 6 and a hysteresis of 2, meaning **on** at 6 and **off** at 4. The last three lines of code are a loop that presents an input voltage increasing from 4 to 7 and back down to 4 each time round the loop "trig1.trigger(v)" is called. This method checks to see if the output for trig1 is low. If it is the switching method is called. Notice that the definition for this method was inherited from class Comparator. If the output of "trig1" is high then the input_voltage is offset by the hysteresis and the switching method called.

The output of this program is shown below. On the way up switching on occurred when the input was greater than 6 and off when 4 was reached on the way down.

```
root@slax:~# python prog_03_02.py
Input voltage = 4.0-----Output = False

Input voltage = 4.5-----Output = False
Input voltage = 5.0-----Output = False
Input voltage = 5.5-----Output = False
Input voltage = 6.0-----Output = False
Input voltage = 6.5-----Output = True
Input voltage = 7.0-----Output = True
Input voltage = 6.5-----Output = True
Input voltage = 6.0-----Output = True
Input voltage = 5.5-----Output = True
Input voltage = 5.0-----Output = True
Input voltage = 4.5-----Output = True
Input voltage = 4.0-----Output = False
root@slax:~#
```

Only one instance of SchmittTrigger was created here but, as before, any number could be used, each with different setpoints or hysteresis values.

3.4 A Practical Data Logger

We will start by considering a data logger that is to receive inputs from several interface devices. Each of these interface devices has eight digital inputs, each input is connected to a switch that is either open on closed. It is required to count the switch closures and log the totals in a "comma separated file" (csv) at regular time intervals along with the time and date, see Fig 3 – 2.

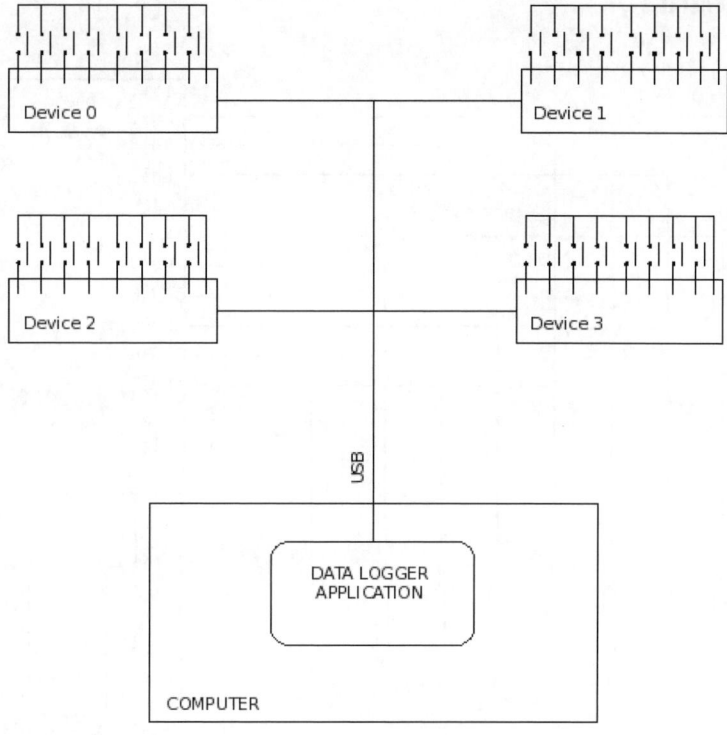

Fig 3 -2

The device that will be used is the UM245R from Future Technologies Development International (FTDI), available from RS Components, In the UK the current price is about twelve pounds and the RS stock number is 406-584. This device is a first in first out (FIFO) parallel register. The eight bits of a single byte can be read from or written to as discrete inputs/outputs. The UM245R is a development board with a type B USB socket on it. It can be configured using jumpers to be bus powered.

3.5 Circuit Board 1

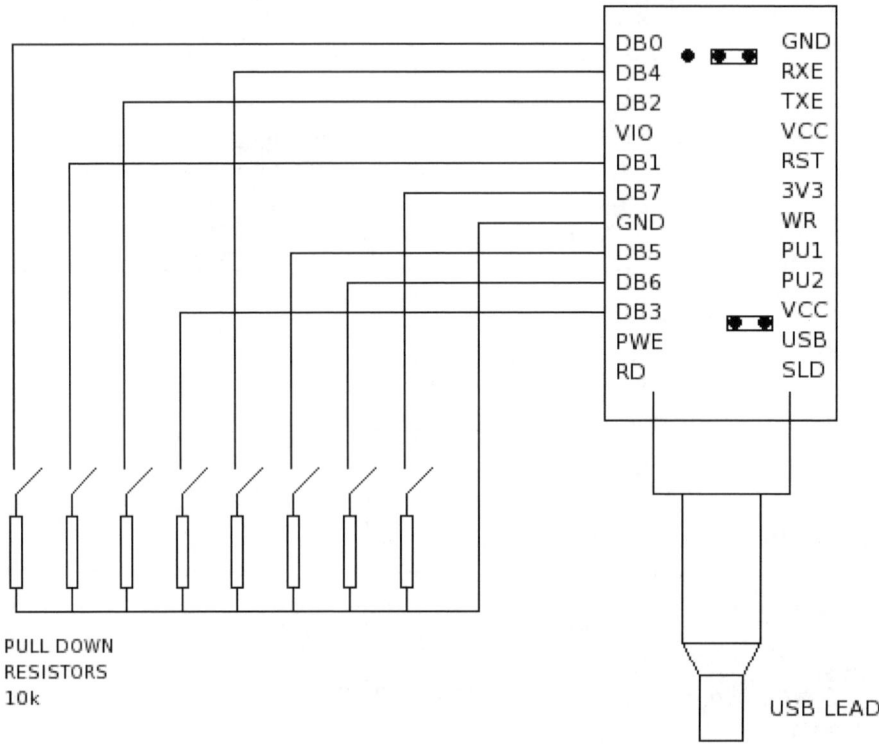

Fig 3 - 3

Now is the time to build a simple hardware project to interface with. Fig 3 - 3 shows the UM245R connected to 8 switches. It is bus powered so no power supply is required. If you use a 24 pin DIL socket the UM245R can be moved from project to project. The easiest way to build it is to use a piece of copper strip matrix board.

Having built the circuit connect it using a USB lead to your computer. Then at an interactive Python prompt type the following.

```
>>> import _simple_ftdi
>>> _simple_ftdi.find_all()
'--Manufacturer: FTDI, Description: UM245R, Serial: FTCVIMKA -- '
```

>>>

The first line imports the module _simple_ftdi, which is a Python binding of seven functions written in 'C'. These functions have been written for this book and are not part of any standard library. They use the libftdi library written by Thomas Jarosch of Intra2net and are provided here as an easy interface for the projects in this book. The source codes for libftdi and simple_ftdi are available on the CD along with a copy of the LGPL 2.1 licence. The second line uses the function "find_all()" which finds all the UM245R devices that are plugged in and returns their serial number, which is actually a string. Below is an example when two devices are present.

```
>>> import _simple_ftdi
>>> _simple_ftdi.find_all()
'--Manufacturer: FTDI, Description: UM245R, Serial: FTCVIMKA -- Manufacturer:
FTDI, Description: UM245R, Serial: FTCVMOYU -- '
>>>
```

Function	1st Argument	2nd Argument	3rd Argument	Return Object
find_all()	-	-	-	String, containing serial numbers of FTDI UM245Rs plugged in.
open_device(...)	String, serial number of FTDI UM245R	Integer, from 0 - 19, handle to device	Integer, from 0 – 255, sets pins as inputs or outputs	Integer, 0 for success, -1 for no device available.
read_pins(.)	Integer, from 0 – 19, device handle	-	-	Integer from 0 – 255, state of the pins.
write_pins(..)	Integer, from 0 – 19, device handle	Integer from 0 – 255, the pins to be set	-	0 if successful negative if not.
ads1286_read(.)	integer, from 0 – 19, device handle	-	-	0 if successful negative if not.
data_get(.)	Integer from 0 - 2	-	-	Integer between 0 – 4095, the analog

				conversion for that input defined by the argument Used after ads1286_read().
close_device(.)	Integer, from 0 – 19, device handle	-	-	None

Table 3 - 1

3.6 A Non-Standard Library of Python Bindings

The seven functions in "_simple_ftdi" are summarized in Table 3 – 1. We will not be using the "write_pins()", "ads1286_read()" and "data_get()" functions until chapter 6.

The serial numbers are used to address the devices for opening. When opening a device you have to give it a number or "handle" from 0 and 19 _simple ftdi allows for up to 20 devices.

The next function to try is the "_simple_ftdi.read_pins(h)" where "h" is the handle, the function returns an integer from 0 and 255.

```
# prog_03_03.py

import _simple_ftdi
from time import sleep
xl = 0

while 1:
    device_up = _simple_ftdi.open_device('FTCVIMKA',0,0)      #Use the serial number for
                                                              #your device, give device
                                               #handle, 0 and set all pins as inputs, 0.

    if device_up == 0:
        x = _simple_ftdi.read_pins(0)              #Reads from device with handle=0.
        if xl != x:
            print x                                #Only prints if the byte read has changed.
            xl = x

        _simple_ftdi.close_device(0)
```

74

```
else:
    print 'Device Missing'
    sleep(1)
```

Prog 3 - 3

Operating the switches with Prog 3 – 3 running will produce an output similar to that shown below. If the correct serial numbered device is present the function open_device() returns 0. If you try and read from a handle that has not been opened the program will crash.

```
root@slax:~# python prog_03_03.py
255
247
254
255
```

Now that we have a hardware device working that generates a byte from binary weighted switches the next thing is to decode this integer back to the individual bits. Prog 3 – 4 does this there are two classes in the program.

The first class is "Device". An instance of this class is created for every device being used. When an instance of this class is created __init__(self, serial) is called where serial is the serial number string passed to it when the instance is created. There are two instances being created here "device"1 and "device2". If you don't have two devices the same serial number can be used for both instances. It will just mean the outputs will be the same.

The first method call in the loop is to read the pins of "device1". In the method "read_device_pins()" the variable "self.pins" is assigned to the integer with the value of the pins. Then a loop steps round eight times each time the value of self.pins tested using the & (bitwise "and" operator) against the value 1. For example suppose the pins were 10000101.

```
      10000101
&     00000001
      00000001
```

This will test if the right-most bit is a 1 or a 0. Here, the answer is 1. This answer is used to set the first member of "self.state".

Next the self.pins is right shifted one place and the right most bit is discarded. Next time round the loop the bitwise test will be this.

75

```
 01000010
& 00000001
 00000000
```

The answer is 0 and is used to set the next member of "self.state". This procedure continues until the state of the individual pins are all reflected by the list "self.state". As there are two instances of class "Device", "device1" and "device2" the above procedure is carried out for both devices.

Going back to the creation of the instances of the classes after the creation of "device1" and device2" an instance of the class "Display", "display" was created. Its argument passed to the "__init__" method is a list of "Device" instances. When the method "display.output()" is called, there is a loop in that method that steps through each member of the list "output.devices" this line is "for n in self.devices". This loop formats a string with the two lists device1.state and device2.state concatenated. This string is only printed if the string has changed since last time.

As well as variables that belong to instances, those that are assigned by "self.", there are also "class variables" that are accessible by all instances. In this program "handle" is a class variable that is initially assigned to '0' and gets incremented every time a device is successfully opened. If a device is successfully opened the function "open_device()" returns '0' other wise '1'. This can be used to alert that the device is missing.

```
# prog_03_04.py
import _simple_ftdi

class Device:
    handle = 0                          #Class variable used as device handle.
    def __init__(self, serial):         #Called for each instance creation.
        self.serial=serial
        self.state=[0, 0, 0, 0, 0, 0, 0, 0]    #Eight member list to hold pin states.
        self.handle = Device.handle
        Device.handle = Device.handle + 1     #Increments for next instance to be created.

    def read_device(self):
        self.device_up = _simple_ftdi.open_device(self.serial, self.handle, 0)    #Opened as all
                                                                                  #inputs
        if self.device_up == 0:
            self.pins = _simple_ftdi.read_pins(self.handle)    #For each device, device1.pins and
```

```python
                                                    #device2.pins.

        for n in range (0, 8):
            self.state[n] = self.pins & 1           #Testing rightmost bit.
            self.pins = self.pins >> 1              #Shifting right one place for next time
                                                    #round the loop.

        _simple_ftdi.close_device(self.handle)

class Display():
    def __init__(self, devices):
        self.devices = devices
        self.s = "
        self.s_last = "

    def output(self):

        self.s = '--'
        for dev in  self.devices:
            if dev.device_up == 0:
                self.s = self.s+str(dev.state) + '--'
            else:
                self.s = self.s + ' Device Missing '

        if self.s_last != self.s:
            print self.s
        self.s_last = self.s

device1 = Device('FTCVIMKA')
device2 = Device('FTCVMOYU')

display = Display([device1, device2])

while 1:
    device1.read_device()
    device2.read_device()
    display.output()
```

Prog 3 – 4

Here is the output for my two devices with all switches closed and then the first four switches of "device1" opened and closed in turn. Then repeated with the program started with "device2" unplugged.

root@slax:~# python prog_03_04.py

--[1, 1, 1, 1, 1, 1, 1, 1]--[1, 1, 1, 1, 1, 1, 1, 1]--
--[0, 1, 1, 1, 1, 1, 1, 1]--[1, 1, 1, 1, 1, 1, 1, 1]--
--[1, 1, 1, 1, 1, 1, 1, 1]--[1, 1, 1, 1, 1, 1, 1, 1]--
--[1, 0, 1, 1, 1, 1, 1, 1]--[1, 1, 1, 1, 1, 1, 1, 1]--
--[1, 1, 1, 1, 1, 1, 1, 1]--[1, 1, 1, 1, 1, 1, 1, 1]--
--[1, 1, 0, 1, 1, 1, 1, 1]--[1, 1, 1, 1, 1, 1, 1, 1]--
--[1, 1, 1, 1, 1, 1, 1, 1]--[1, 1, 1, 1, 1, 1, 1, 1]--
--[1, 1, 1, 0, 1, 1, 1, 1]--[1, 1, 1, 1, 1, 1, 1, 1]--
--[1, 1, 1, 1, 1, 1, 1, 1]--[1, 1, 1, 1, 1, 1, 1, 1]--

root@slax:~# python prog_03_04.py
--[1, 1, 1, 1, 1, 1, 1, 1]--No Device--
--[0, 1, 1, 1, 1, 1, 1, 1]--No Device--
--[1, 1, 1, 1, 1, 1, 1, 1]--No Device--
--[1, 0, 1, 1, 1, 1, 1, 1]--No Device--
--[1, 1, 1, 1, 1, 1, 1, 1]--No Device--
--[1, 1, 0, 1, 1, 1, 1, 1]--No Device--
--[1, 1, 1, 1, 1, 1, 1, 1]--No Device--
--[1, 1, 1, 0, 1, 1, 1, 1]--No Device--
--[1, 1, 1, 1, 1, 1, 1, 1]--No Device--

Below Fig 3 – 4 shows how the instances are created from the class definitions for Prog 3 – 3.

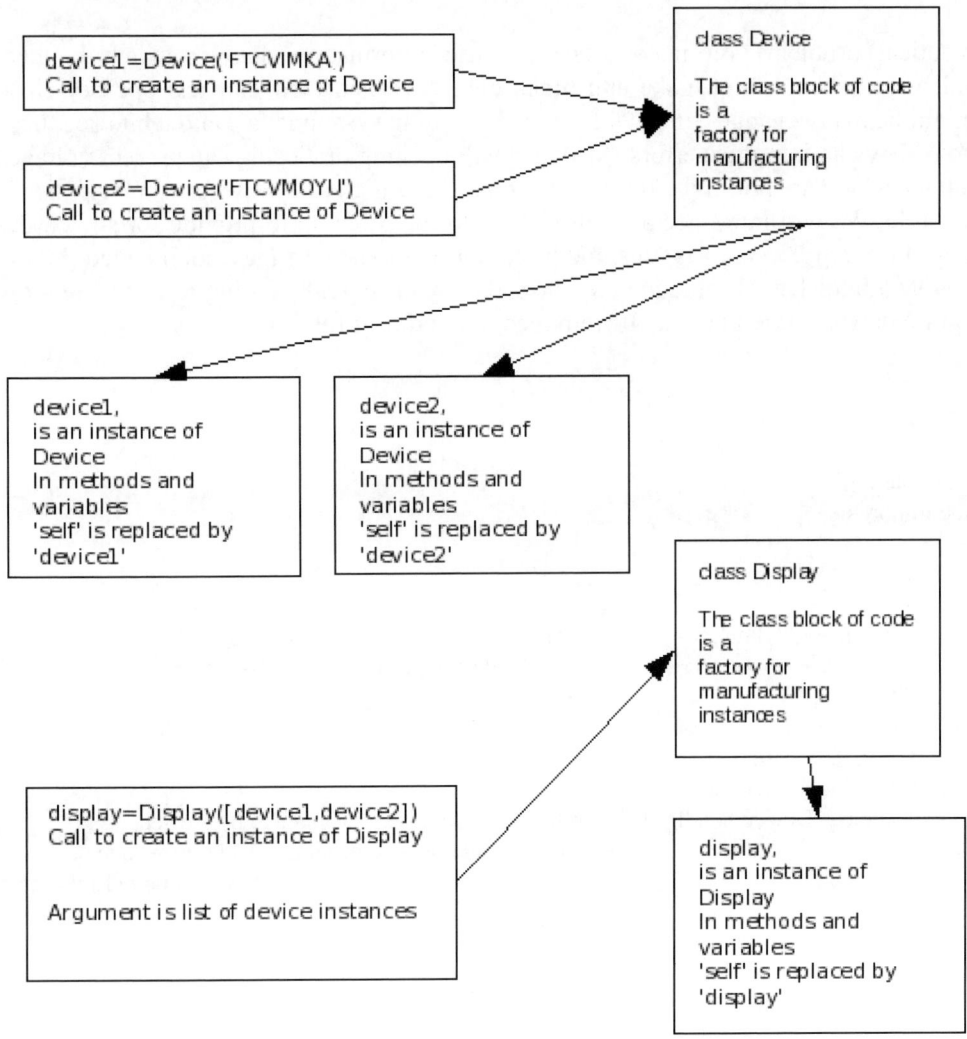

Fig. 3 – 4

More devices can be handled by just creating more instances, adding them to the "display.devices" list and calling the methods.

3.7 Switch De-Bounce

One practical problem you may notice is false information due to switch bounce. Mechanical switches do not make and break cleanly. When their contacts open or close there might be many changes of state. If the data logging system is fast enough to see these transitions they can introduce errors. Also a switch opening or closing can present voltages to the inputs which are not in the range for a guaranteed high or low, where the response is unpredictable. We will introduce a small change to the program to provide for switch de-bouncing. Program 3 – 5 has this modification with the changes commented in the program. Two lines have been added to show the "bounce_reg" shifting right and to slow the program down. These lines can be removed to operate at full speed.

```
# prog_03_05.py

import _simple_ftdi
from time import sleep

class Device():
    handle = 0
    def __init__(self, serial, bounce):        #Argument added 'bounce' an integer to
                                               #set the de-bounce count.

        self.serial = serial
        self.bounce = bounce
        self.state=[0, 0, 0, 0, 0, 0, 0, 0]
        self.handle = Device.handle
        Device.handle = Device.handle+1        #Increments for next instance to be created.
                                               #List of intergers with value self.bounce, one for each
                                               #pin. The '\' allows a long line to continue onto the next
                                               #line.

        self.bounce_reg = [self.bounce, self.bounce, self.bounce, \
        self.bounce, self.bounce, self.bounce, self.bounce, self.bounce]


    def read_device(self):
        self.device_up = _simple_ftdi.open_device(self.serial, self.handle, 0)
        if self.device_up == 0:
            self.pins = _simple_ftdi.read_pins(self.handle)
            sleep(1)                           #To slow the program down.
            print self.bounce_reg              #To view the registers.
            for n in range (0, 8):
```

```python
            if self.pins & 1 == 0:
                self.bounce_reg[n] = self.bounce_reg[n] >> 1
            else:
                self.bounce_reg[n] = self.bounce

            if self.bounce_reg[n] == 0:
                self.state[n] = 0
            else:
                self.state[n] = 1

            self.pins = self.pins >> 1

        _simple_ftdi.close_device(self.handle)


class Display():
    def __init__(self, devices):
        self.devices = devices
        self.s = ''
        self.s_last = ''

    def output(self):

        self.s='--'
        for dev in  self.devices:
            if dev.device_up == 0:
                self.s = self.s+str(dev.state)+'--'
            else:
                self.s = self.s + ' Device Missing '

        if self.s_last != self.s:
            print self.s
        self.s_last=self.s
device1 = Device('FTCVIMKA', 4096)  # 2^1
display = Display([device1])


while 1:
    device1.read_device()
    display.output()
```

Prog 3 – 5

There is a list of integers called "self.bounce_reg". Each member of the list is assigned to an initial integer "self.bounce"; there is a member for each input pin of the device. When a pin is read and seen to be '0' the member of the list for that pin is right shifted. If the pin subsequently goes to '1' the member of "self.bounce_reg" for that pin immediately goes back to its initial value. Only when all of the bits have been shifted right and off the end does the "self.state" for that pin get set. So if you want four reads before the output string changes the value for "self.bounce" would be 8. Incidentally it would give the same result as 15 or any value between because it would be the same number of places to be shifted.

8 = 1000 Four places to be shifted right to reach zero.

15 =1111 Four place to be shifted right to reach zero.

Below is the result of opening switch 0 then closing it. The number 4096 which is 1000000000000 binary was used. The value for self.bounce_reg[0] had to be shifted 13 time before a change of state occurred, opening the switch causes an immediate change of state.

--[1, 1, 1, 1, 1, 1, 1, 0]--

[4096, 4096, 4096, 4096, 4096, 4096, 4096, 0]   #Bounce register values with
                                                       #switch 0 closed

[4096, 4096, 4096, 4096, 4096, 4096, 4096, 0]
[4096, 4096, 4096, 4096, 4096, 4096, 4096, 0]
[4096, 4096, 4096, 4096, 4096, 4096, 4096, 0]
[4096, 4096, 4096, 4096, 4096, 4096, 4096, 0]

--[1, 1, 1, 1, 1, 1, 1, 1]--   #Switch opens

[4096, 4096, 4096, 4096, 4096, 4096, 4096, 4096]   #Switch closes
[4096, 4096, 4096, 4096, 4096, 4096, 4096, 2048]
[4096, 4096, 4096, 4096, 4096, 4096, 4096, 1024]
[4096, 4096, 4096, 4096, 4096, 4096, 4096, 512]
[4096, 4096, 4096, 4096, 4096, 4096, 4096, 256]
[4096, 4096, 4096, 4096, 4096, 4096, 4096, 128]
[4096, 4096, 4096, 4096, 4096, 4096, 4096, 64]
[4096, 4096, 4096, 4096, 4096, 4096, 4096, 32]
[4096, 4096, 4096, 4096, 4096, 4096, 4096, 16]
[4096, 4096, 4096, 4096, 4096, 4096, 4096, 8]
[4096, 4096, 4096, 4096, 4096, 4096, 4096, 4]
[4096, 4096, 4096, 4096, 4096, 4096, 4096, 2]
[4096, 4096, 4096, 4096, 4096, 4096, 4096, 1]

--[1, 1, 1, 1, 1, 1, 1, 0]--   #13 right shifts with the switch
                                                       #closed

[4096, 4096, 4096, 4096, 4096, 4096, 4096, 0]

```
# prog_03_06.py

import _simple_ftdi

class Device:
    handle=0
    def __init__(self, serial, bounce):
        self.serial = serial
        self.bounce = bounce
        self.state = [0, 0, 0, 0, 0, 0, 0, 0]
        self.device_up = _simple_ftdi.open_device(self.serial, Device.handle, 0)
        self.handle = Device.handle
        Device.handle = Device.handle + 1          #Increments for next instance to be created.
        self.bounce_reg = [self.bounce, self.bounce, self.bounce, \
        self.bounce, self.bounce, self.bounce, self.bounce, self.bounce]
        self.accumulator = [0, 0, 0, 0, 0, 0, 0, 0]          #Accumulator is a list of integers.
        self.last_state = [0, 0, 0, 0, 0, 0, 0, 0]          #Another new list to hold previous
                                                            #state of the pin.
    def read_device(self):
        self.device_up = _simple_ftdi.open_device(self.serial, self.handle, 0)

        if self.device_up == 0:
            self.pins = _simple_ftdi.read_pins(self.handle)

            for n in range (0, 8):

                if self.pins & 1 == 0:
                    self.bounce_reg[n] = self.bounce_reg[n]  >> 1
                else:
                    self.bounce_reg[n]=self.bounce

                if self.bounce_reg[n] == 0:
                    self.state[n] = 0
                else:
                    self.state[n] = 1

                self.pins = self.pins >> 1

                if self.state[n] == 1 and  self.last_state[n] == 0:
                    self.accumulator[n] = self.accumulator[n] + 1

                self.last_state[n] = self.state[n]
```

```
        _simple_ftdi.close_device(self.handle)



class Display:
    def __init__(self, devices):
        self.devices = devices
        self.s_last = "
    def output(self):
        s = "
        for dev in  self.devices:
            s = s + ' Handle'
            s = s+str(dev.handle) + ' --> '
            if dev.device_up==0:
                s = s+str(dev.state) + str(dev.accumulator)
            else:
                s = s + 'Device Missing'

        if self.s_last != s:
            print s

        self.s_last = s

device1 = Device('FTCVIMKA',8)
device2 = Device('FTCVMOYU',8)
display = Display([device1,device2])

while 1:
    device1.read_device()
    device2.read_device()
    display.output()
```

Prog 3 – 6

Program 3 – 6 above adds an accumulator to count the number of switch closures. Prog 3 - 7 adds a class to log the results at regular intervals with a time stamp to a "csv" file which can be opened with a spread sheet program. Fig 3 – 5 below shows the UM245R connected to push switches.

Later in this book the class "Device" will be altered slightly and put in a file with other classes as "DeviceA" to make a module of reusable code.

```
# prog_03_07.py
import _simple_ftdi
import time

class Device:
    handle = 0
    def __init__(self, serial, bounce):
        self.serial = serial
        self.bounce = bounce
        self.state = [0, 0, 0, 0, 0, 0, 0, 0]
        self.handle = Device.handle
        Device.handle = Device.handle+1
        self.bounce_reg = [self.bounce, self.bounce, self.bounce,\
        self.bounce, self.bounce, self.bounce, self.bounce, self.bounce]
        self.accumulator = [0, 0, 0, 0, 0, 0, 0, 0]
        self.last_state = [0, 0, 0, 0, 0, 0, 0, 0]

    def read_device(self):
        self.device_up = _simple_ftdi.open_device(self.serial, self.handle, 0)

        if self.device_up == 0:
            self.pins = _simple_ftdi.read_pins(self.handle)

            for n in range (0, 8):

                if self.pins & 1==0:
                    self.bounce_reg[n] = self.bounce_reg[n] >> 1
                else:
                    self.bounce_reg[n] = self.bounce

                if self.bounce_reg[n] == 0:
                    self.state[n] = 0
                else:
                    self.state[n] = 1

                self.pins = self.pins >> 1

                if self.state[n] == 1 and  self.last_state[n] == 0:
                    self.accumulator[n] = self.accumulator[n] + 1

                self.last_state[n] = self.state[n]

            _simple_ftdi.close_device(self.handle)
```

85

```python
class Display:
    def __init__(self,devices):
        self.devices=devices
        self.s_last = ''
    def output(self):
        s = ''
        for dev in  self.devices:
            s = s + ' Handle'
            s = s+str(dev.handle) + ' --> '
            if dev.device_up==0:
                s=s+str(dev.state)+str(dev.accumulator)
            else:
                s = s+'Device Missing'

        if self.s_last != s:
            print s

        self.s_last = s
class Log:
    def __init__(self,devices,display,period):
        t=time.localtime()

        self.file_name = str(t[0]) + str(t[1]) + '_' + str(t[2]) +'_' +\
            str(t[3]) + '_' + str(t[4]) + '_' + str(t[5]) + '.csv'
        print self.file_name
        self.devices = devices
        self.period = period
        self.display = display
        f = open(self.file_name,'w')
        header = 'Time,'

        for h in range (0, 8*len(devices)):
            header = header+'Input ' + str(h) + ','
        header = header + '\n'
        f.write(header)
        f.close
        self.last_time = time.time()

    def logging(self):
        if time.time() - self.last_time > self.period:
```

```
    line = time.asctime()+ ','
    for dev in self.devices:
        for bit in range (0,8):
            if dev.device_up == 0:
                line = line + str(dev.accumulator[bit]) + ','
            else:
                line = line + 'Device Missing,'


    f=open(self.file_name,'a')
    line = line + '\n'
    f.write(line)
    print time.asctime() +' Logging'
    f.close()
    self.last_time = time.time()

device1 = Device('FTCVIMKA',8)
device2 = Device('FTCVMOYU',8)
display = Display([device1,device2])
log = Log([device1, device2], [display], 10)
while 1:
    device1.read_device()
    device2.read_device()
    display.output()
    log.logging()
```

Prog 3 – 7

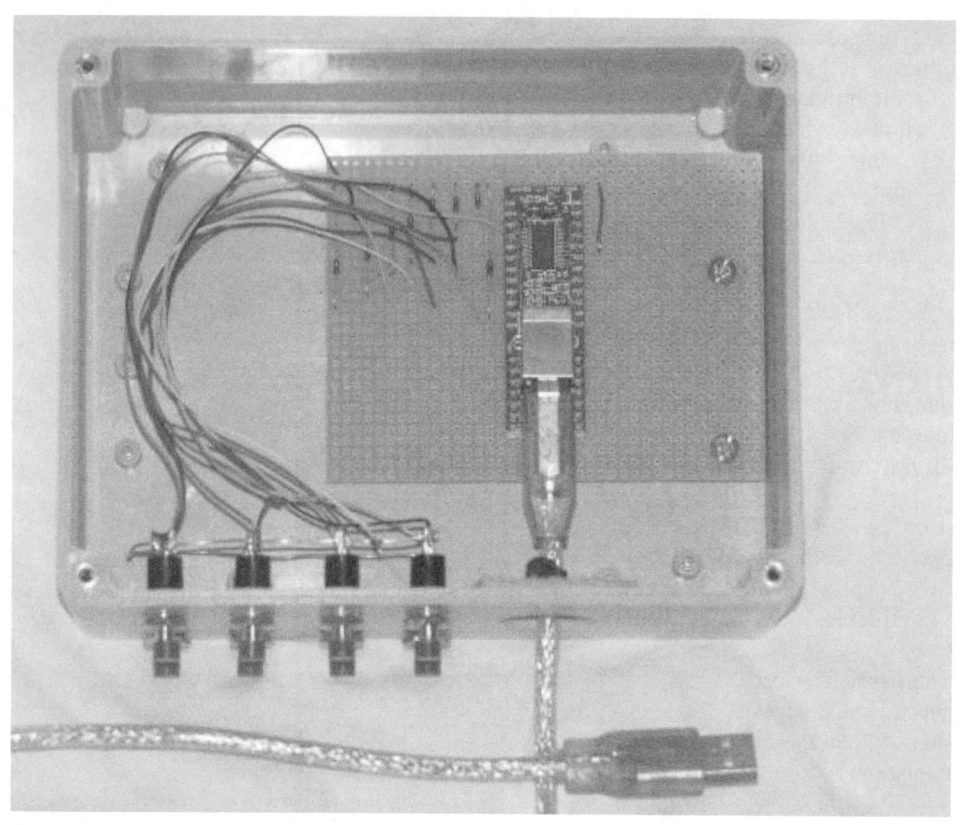

Fig 3 – 5

Chapter 4

Graphic User Interfaces

4.1 Introduction

As far as functionality is concerned, adequate programs can be written with just the command line as an interface. However, a graphical interface is a much more attractive proposition, offering the usual "widgets" that most computer users are used to using, buttons, check buttons, radio buttons, etc.. Python offers a simple way of creating these interfaces for your programs. One of the projects that will be developed through this chapter will be a mimic of an analogue meter having a realistic, damped needle movement. As has been mentioned before, there is not an intention of trying to treat any of the topics in utmost depth but, rather, to give the reader a set of useful introductory tools to build projects that work and give pointers to further learning.

4.2 Tkinter

Tkinter is the standard library that provides Python bindings to Tk that is a graphical programming library. Tkinter offers a great deal of variety, I have presented a few example programs that do not by any means cover all what is available. I would recommend running the example programs and experimenting with them to suit you. The widgets that make up the interface have attributes with particular names, some are in the example programs.

We will start by creating the simplest graphical program that creates an empty window and then does nothing other resize, minimize, maximise and close. These three lines of code actually do a lot of work.

```
#prog_04_01

from Tkinter import *        #This imports Tkinter's entire namespace,
                             #we can call Tkinter's variables and methods without
                             #having to type 'Tkinter.some_method()' we just type
                             #'some_method()'
root = Tk()                  #Tk() is the top level class.
root.mainloop()              #Mainloop is the  loop that responds to events like button clicks.
```

Prog 4 – 1

4.3 Grid Layout

In the "__init__()" function of the class the widgets we want are given names. The actual names you choose are up to you but it helps if they are descriptive and follow a logical pattern. The first button name is called "self.but_on" and is assigned to the class Button. In the parenthesis of the widget classes you set options that set their appearance and behaviour. There is a set of attributes for each widget. The buttons here have their text attribute set. The canvas widgets have their size, this is in pixels, and their background colour set. Just creating the widgets will not make them appear; you have to use one of the layout managers. We will just use one method, the grid() method. This is easy to use and is similar to what we will be doing with laying out web pages with "html" in chapter 9. The grid method of layout is actually quite flexible and allows widgets to span more than one column or row, also by using padding cells can be bigger than their widget. See Fig 4 – 1 and Fig. 4 – 2 to see how this all works.

```
#prog_04_02.py

from Tkinter import *

class FrontEnd():
    def __init__(self, master):
        self.master = master
        self.master.title('Heater Controller')    #Sets the window title.
        self.but_on = Button(text='ON')           #The following lines create instances of widgets.
        self.but_off = Button(text='OFF')
        self.can_on_lamp = Canvas(width = 40, height = 40, bg = 'grey')
        self.can_off_lamp = Canvas(width = 40, height = 40, bg = 'red')
        self.lab_heater_switch = Label(text = 'HEATER\nSWITCH')    #Note '/n' character to create
                                                                   #newline in label text.
        self.lab_heater_on = Label(text = 'ON')
        self.lab_heater_off = Label(text = 'OFF')

                                                                   #Layout starts here.
        self.lab_heater_switch.grid(row = 0, column = 0, columnspan = 2)   #This label spans
                                                                   #two columns.
        self.lab_heater_off.grid(row=0,column = 2, sticky = 'S')   #Sticky='S' offsets
                                                                   #the label to the
                                                                   #bottom of the cell.
        self.lab_heater_on.grid(row = 0, column = 3, sticky = 'S')
        self.but_off.grid(row = 1, column = 0, sticky = 'NW')
        self.but_on.grid(row = 1, column = 1, sticky = 'SE')
        self.can_off_lamp.grid(row = 1, column = 2, padx =10, pady =10)    #Canvas has 10
```

90

```
        self.can_on_lamp.grid(row = 1, column = 3, padx = 10, pady = 10)
```

```
#pixels padding top
#and sides
#to make the cell
#bigger.
```

```
root = Tk()
frontend = FrontEnd(root)
root.mainloop()
```

Prog 4 – 2

In the "__init__()" function of the class the widgets we want are given names, the names you choose are up to you but it helps if they are descriptive and follow a logical pattern. The first button name is called "self.but_on" and is assigned to the class Button. In the parenthesis of the widget classes you set options that set their appearance and behaviour. There is a set of attributes for each widget. The buttons here have their text attribute set. The canvas widgets have their size, this is in pixels, and their background colour set. Just creating the widgets will not make them appear, you have to use one of the layout managers. We will just use one method, the grid() method. This is easy to use and is similar to what we will be doing with laying out web pages with "html" in chapter 9. The grid method of layout is actually quite flexible and allows widgets to span more than one column or row, also by using padding cells can be bigger than their widget. See Fig 4 – 1 and Fig. 4 – 2 to see how this all works.

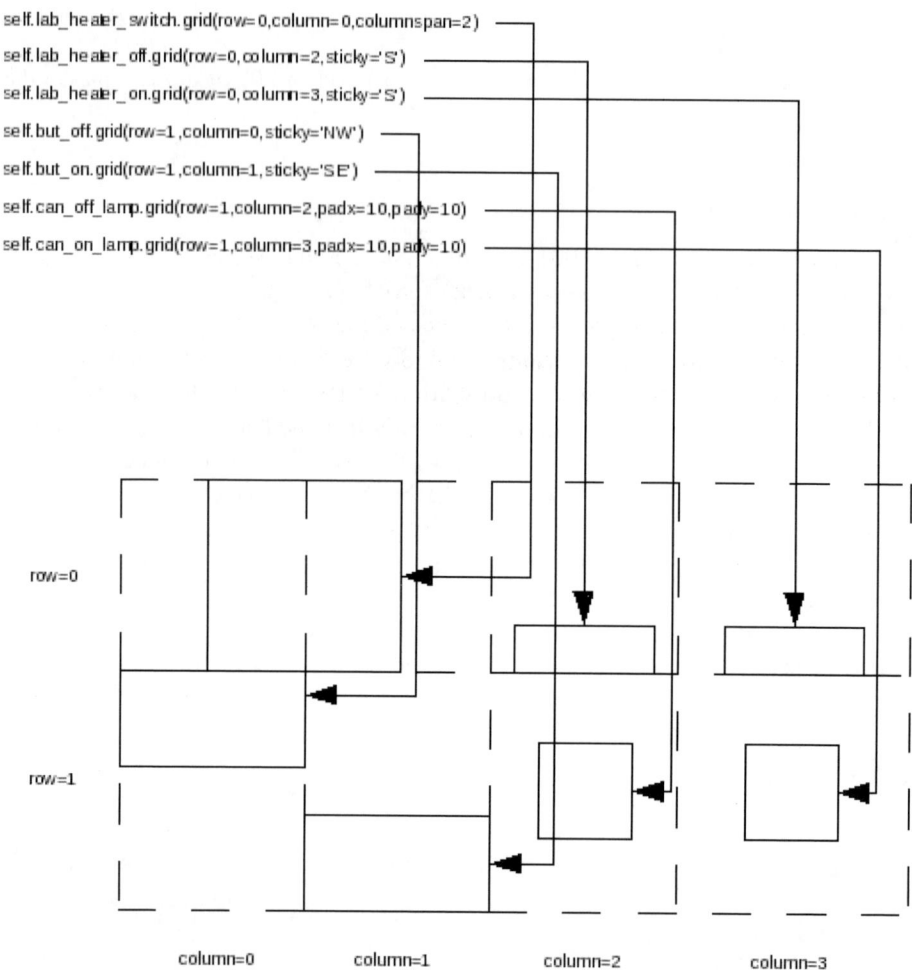

self.lab_heater_switch.grid(row=0,column=0,columnspan=2)

self.lab_heater_off.grid(row=0,column=2,sticky='S')

self.lab_heater_on.grid(row=0,column=3,sticky='S')

self.but_off.grid(row=1,column=0,sticky='NW')

self.but_on.grid(row=1,column=1,sticky='SE')

self.can_off_lamp.grid(row=1,column=2,padx=10,pady=10)

self.can_on_lamp.grid(row=1,column=3,padx=10,pady=10)

row=0

row=1

column=0   column=1   column=2   column=3

Fig. 4 – 1

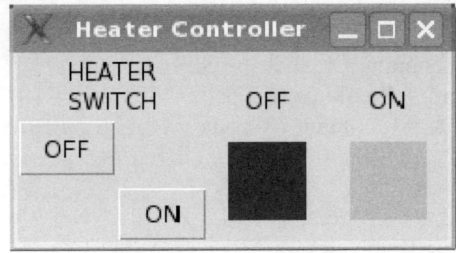

Fig. 4 – 2

4.4 Callbacks

If you run the program and click on the buttons you will notice that nothing happens. What is needed is an addition to the button's options called "command" which will cause something to happen. Prog 4 – 3 has two methods "on()" and "off()" which change the background colour of the canvas widgets, using the ".configure()" method. Notice that the "command = self.on" and "command = self.off" expressions do not end with parenthesis. This is because they are what are called, callbacks. They call to Tkinter to call the actual methods when the button is clicked. If you put parenthesis after them they would attempt to call the methods as the "frontend" instance was being created, which is not what is wanted.

```
#prog_04_03
from Tkinter import *

class FrontEnd():
    def __init__(self, master):
        self.master = master
        self.master.title('Heater Controller')
        self.but_on = Button(text = 'ON',command = self.on)
        self.but_off = Button(text ='OFF',command = self.off)
        self.can_on_lamp = Canvas(width = 40,height = 40,bg = 'grey')
        self.can_off_lamp = Canvas(width = 40,height = 40,bg = 'red')
        self.lab_heater_switch = Label(text = 'HEATER\nSWITCH')
        self.lab_heater_on = Label(text = 'ON')
        self.lab_heater_off = Label(text = 'OFF')

        self.lab_heater_switch.grid(row = 0, column = 0, columnspan = 2)
        self.lab_heater_off.grid(row = 0, column = 2, sticky = 'S')
```

93

```
    self.lab_heater_on.grid(row = 0, column = 3, sticky ='S')
    self.but_off.grid(row = 1, column = 0, sticky = 'NW')
    self.but_on.grid(row = 1, column = 1, sticky = 'SE')
    self.can_off_lamp.grid(row = 1, column = 2, padx = 10, pady = 10)
    self.can_on_lamp.grid(row = 1, column =3, padx = 10, pady = 10)

  def on(self):
    self.can_on_lamp.configure(bg = 'green')
    self.can_off_lamp.configure(bg = 'grey')

  def off(self):
    self.can_off_lamp.configure(bg='red')
    self.can_on_lamp.configure(bg='grey')

root = Tk()
frontend = FrontEnd(root)
root.mainloop()
```

Prog 4 – 3

There is something different about the way our GUI programs run compared with previous command line programs. The GUI program is event driven. The mainloop() is constantly checking to see if an event such as a mouse click has happened. For this to work we must avoid writing functions that block, meaning they stop, waiting for one particular thing to happen like the "raw_input()" method, or the sleep() method. Suppose we want the heater controller to turn off automatically after 10 seconds, we can do this with the ".after()' method as in Prog. 4 – 5. The second argument of this method is the function or method called after a delay specified by the first argument in milliseconds. This function and the mainloop function run together, so no blocking occurs.

```
#prog_04_04

from Tkinter import *

class FrontEnd():
    def __init__(self,master):
        self.master = master
        self.master.title('Heater Controller')
        self.but_on = Button(text = 'ON', command = self.on)
        self.but_off = Button(text = 'OFF', command = self.off)
        self.can_on_lamp = Canvas(width = 40, height = 40, bg = 'grey')
        self.can_off_lamp = Canvas(width = 40, height = 40, bg = 'red')
        self.can_dwell_lamp = Canvas(width = 40, height = 40, bg = 'yellow')
        self.lab_heater_switch = Label(text = 'HEATER\nSWITCH')
        self.lab_heater_on = Label(text = 'ON')
        self.lab_heater_off = Label(text = 'OFF')

        self.lab_heater_switch.grid(row = 0, column = 0, columnspan = 2)
        self.lab_heater_off.grid(row = 0, column = 2, sticky = 'S')
        self.lab_heater_on.grid(row = 0, column = 3, sticky = 'S')
        self.but_off.grid(row = 1, column = 0, sticky = 'NW')
        self.but_on.grid(row = 1, column = 1, sticky = 'SE')
        self.can_off_lamp.grid(row = 1, column = 2, padx = 10, pady = 10)
        self.can_on_lamp.grid(row = 1, column = 3, padx =10, pady = 10)

    def on(self):
        self.can_on_lamp.configure(bg = 'green')
        self.can_off_lamp.configure(bg = 'grey')
        self.master.after(10000, self.off)            #The .after(10000,self.off)
                                                      #calls self.off after 10000 milliseconds.

    def off(self):
        self.can_off_lamp.configure(bg = 'red')
        self.can_on_lamp.configure(bg = 'grey')

root = Tk()
frontend = FrontEnd(root)
root.mainloop()
```

Prog 4 – 4

In order for the program to switch a heater on and off there has to be an actual hardware interface. The "_simple_ftdi" library has three functions "find_all()" to identify devices plugged in, "read_pins()", and write_pins(). The write_pins() is the function used to control output from the devices. As this chapter is about Tkinter we will leave actual hardware interfacing for writing to the pins until chapter 6.

4.5 Inputting Data With The Scale Widget

In chapter 2 we used the function "raw_input()" to read the keyboard buffer. With a GUI you have much better ways of inputting data. Remember, we do not want the program to block waiting for one thing to happen; we want the eventloop to be watching for all events. GUIs offer a range of ways to input data.

The first method to look at is the "Scale" widget. A scale widget allows you to input numerical data by dragging the position of a slider. Prog. 4 – 5 shows a simple program that has a "Scale" widget and a "Label" widget. The attributes set when creating this widget here are "horizontal" , default is vertical, the length, the variable, and a callback whenever the scale is moved. When the scale is moved with the mouse, the callback causes method cx_lab1(self,x) to be called. Tkinter passes this method for which we have written two arguments - one is the instance "frontend" that is self, and the other is a string representing the position of the scale that is the variable "s". The attribute "resolution" has been set to 0.1, which is a float. The default, if no resolution is set, is for an integer. In the method, "s" is used to change the text of the label "lab1", and then converted to a float for comparison with 80. If the scale is higher than 80 the background of the label is set to red; otherwise it is green.


```
#prog_04_05

from Tkinter import *

class FrontEnd():
    def __init__(self, master):
        self.master = master
        self.master.title('Scale Widget')
        self.scale1 = Scale(orient = 'horizontal', length = 500,\
        resolution = 0.1, command = self.cx_lab1)
        self.lab1 = Label(bg = 'green')

        self.lab1.grid(row = 0, column = 0)
        self.scale1.grid(row = 1, column = 0)

    def cx_lab1(self, s):
        self.lab1.configure(text = s)
```

```
        if float(s) > 80:
            self.lab1.configure(bg ='red')
        else:
            self.lab1.configure(bg ='green')

root = Tk()
frontend = FrontEnd(root)
root.mainloop()
```

Prog 4 – 5

Other useful attributes of the scale widget are the "from_" and "to" which set the end values of the scale. The underscore after from is there because "from" is a Python keyword. The scale can be decorated with markers with the "tickinterval" attribute which puts graduations on the scale.

```
#prog_04_06
from Tkinter import *

class FrontEnd():
    def __init__(self, master):
        self.master = master
        self.master.title('Scale Widget')
        self.scale1 = Scale(orient = 'horizontal', length = 500, resolution = 0.1, \
        command = self.cx_lab1,from_ = 20, to = 90, tickinterval = 10)
        self.lab1 = Label(bg = 'green')

        self.lab1.grid(row = 0, column = 0)
        self.scale1.grid(row = 1, column = 0)

    def cx_lab1(self, s):
        self.lab1.configure(text = s)
        if float(s) > 80:
            self.lab1.configure(bg = 'red')
        else:
            self.lab1.configure(bg = 'green')

root = Tk()
frontend = FrontEnd(root)
root.mainloop()
```

Prog 4 – 6

97

4.6 Control Variables

Behind some widgets are values that can represent strings, floats, or integers. In order for widgets to share values there is a special container called a control variable. In Prog 4 - 7 a variable with invented name "self.contvar1" is an instance of a StringVar() which is a type string control variable. In the program the scale widget has its variable assigned to "self.contvar1" and the textvariable for the label "lab1" also is assigned to "self.contvar1". Whenever the scale changes the "self.contvar1" changes, and this changes the text of the label.

```
#prog_04_07

from Tkinter import *

class FrontEnd():
    def __init__(self, master):
        self.master = master
        self.master.title('Scale Widget, Label Widget and Shared Control Varaible')
        self.contvar1 = StringVar()                          #Control variable

        self.scale1 = Scale(orient = 'horizontal', length = 500,\
        resolution = 0.1, variable = self.contvar1)          #Shared control variable
        self.lab1 = Label(bg = 'green', textvariable = self.contvar1)   #Shared control variable

        self.lab1.grid(row = 0, column = 0)
        self.scale1.grid(row = 1,column = 0)

root=Tk()
frontend = FrontEnd(root)
root.mainloop()
```

Prog 4 – 7

The next program uses a control variable type IntVar(), which is an integer. Control variables have two methods ".set()" and ".get()". This program uses ".set()" to move the scale to indicate the binary value of the pins of an FTDI device.

```
#prog_04_08
from Tkinter import *
import _simple_ftdi
```

98

```
class FrontEnd():
    def __init__(self, master):
        self.master = master
        self.master.title('Analog Input')
        self.contvar1 = IntVar()

        self.scale1 = Scale(orient = 'horizontal', length = 500,\
        variable =self.contvar1, to = 255, tickinterval = 50,bg = 'black')

        self.scale1.grid()
        self.poll()

    def poll(self):
        device_up = _simple_ftdi.open_device('FTCVIMKA',0,0)       #Use you device's
                                                                    #serial number.

        if device_up == 0:
            x = _simple_ftdi.read_pins(0)
            _simple_ftdi.close_device(0)
            self.contvar1.set(x)
            self.scale1.configure(label = 'Device Present', fg = 'green')   #Green text if
                                                                            #device present.
        else:
            self.scale1.configure(label = 'No Device!',fg = 'red')          #Warns if there is
                                                                            #no device, with red text.

        self.master.after(5, self.poll)                            #Reads the pins every
                                                                    #5 microseconds.
root = Tk()
frontend = FrontEnd(root)

root.mainloop()
```

Prog 4 – 8

With Prog. 4 - 8 if you try and move the scale with the mouse it will spring back to its set position. If you built the interface described in chapter 3, then plug it in, but make sure you have amended the serial number for your device. The scale will move to the binary values you input on your switches. If the device with the correct serial number is not there a warning is given, and the text turns red.

4.7 Inputting Data Using The Check Buttons

Check buttons allow the user to pick items by ticking boxes with the mouse. Prog 4 – 9 is a variation on the simple heater controller where we can switch the heater on and off, except here there are three separate heater elements. Which elements switch on depends on which check boxes are ticked. Each check button has a different control variable, which is an "IntVar()". When a box is ticked its IntVar() is 1 and when it is un-ticked its IntVar() is 0.

```
#prog_04_09
from Tkinter import *

class FrontEnd():
    def __init__(self, master):
        self.master = master
        self.master.title('Heater Controller ')

        self.intvar_heater1 = IntVar()
        self.intvar_heater2 = IntVar()
        self.intvar_heater3 = IntVar()

        self.but_on = Button(text='ON', command = self.on)
        self.but_off = Button(text='OFF', command = self.off)

        self.can_lamp1 = Canvas(width = 40, height = 40, bg = 'red')
        self.can_lamp2 = Canvas(width = 40, height = 40, bg = 'red')
        self.can_lamp3 = Canvas(width = 40, height = 40, bg = 'red')

        self.lab_heater_switch = Label(text = 'HEATER\nSWITCH')
        self.lab_heater_on = Label(text = 'ON')
        self.lab_heater_off = Label(text = 'OFF')

        self.check1 = Checkbutton(text = 'Element 1',variable = self.intvar_heater1)
        self.check2 = Checkbutton(text = 'Element 2',variable = self.intvar_heater2)
        self.check3 = Checkbutton(text = 'Element 3',variable = self.intvar_heater3)

        self.lab_heater_switch.grid(row = 0, column = 0, columnspan = 2)
        self.but_off.grid(row = 1, column = 0, sticky = 'NW')
        self.but_on.grid(row = 1, column = 1, sticky = 'SE')
        self.can_lamp1.grid(row = 1, column = 2, padx =10, pady = 10)
        self.can_lamp2.grid(row = 1, column = 3, padx = 10, pady = 10)
        self.can_lamp3.grid(row = 1, column = 4, padx = 10, pady = 10)
```

```python
      self.check1.grid(row = 2, column = 0)
      self.check2.grid(row = 3, column = 0)
      self.check3.grid(row = 4, column = 0)

   def on(self):
      if self.intvar_heater1.get():
         self.can_lamp1.configure(bg = 'green')
      if self.intvar_heater2.get():
         self.can_lamp2.configure(bg = 'green')
      if self.intvar_heater3.get():
         self.can_lamp3.configure(bg = 'green')

   def off(self):
      self.can_lamp1.configure(bg = 'red')
      self.can_lamp2.configure(bg = 'red')
      self.can_lamp3.configure(bg = 'red')

root = Tk()
frontend = FrontEnd(root)

root.mainloop()
```

Prog 4 – 9

4.8 Inputting Data Using The Radio Buttons

Radio buttons are similar to check buttons except that only one choice is available in any group of buttons.
To group buttons you simple give them the same control variable. Each button then sets the control variable to a different value when it is selected.


```python
#prog_04_10

from Tkinter import *

class FrontEnd():
   def __init__(self, master):
      self.master = master
      self.master.title('Heater Controller ')

      self.intvar_heater = IntVar()
```

```python
        self.but_on = Button(text = 'ON', command = self.on)
        self.but_off=Button(text = 'OFF', command = self.off)

        self.can_lamp1 = Canvas(width = 40, height = 40, bg = 'red')
        self.can_lamp2 = Canvas(width = 40, height = 40, bg = 'red')
        self.can_lamp3 = Canvas(width = 40, height = 40, bg = 'red')

        self.lab_heater_switch = Label(text = 'HEATER\nSWITCH')
        self.lab_heater_on = Label(text = 'ON')
        self.lab_heater_off = Label(text = 'OFF')

        self.rad1 = Radiobutton(text = 'Element 1', variable = self.intvar_heater, value = 1) #All have
                                                              #the same control variable.
        self.rad2 = Radiobutton(text = 'Element 2', variable = self.intvar_heater, value = 2) #Value is
                                                              #the value of the control
                                                              #variable.
        self.rad3 = Radiobutton(text = 'Element 3', variable = self.intvar_heater, value = 3)

        self.lab_heater_switch.grid(row = 0, column = 0, columnspan = 2)
        self.but_off.grid(row = 1, column = 0, sticky ='NW')
        self.but_on.grid(row = 1, column = 1, sticky = 'SE')
        self.can_lamp1.grid(row =1,column = 2, padx = 10, pady = 10)
        self.can_lamp2.grid(row = 1, column = 3, padx = 10, pady = 10)
        self.can_lamp3.grid(row = 1, column = 4, padx = 10, pady = 10)
        self.rad1.grid(row = 2, column = 0)
        self.rad2.grid(row = 3, column = 0)
        self.rad3.grid(row= 4, column = 0)

    def on(self):
        if self.intvar_heater.get() == 1:
            self.can_lamp1.configure(bg = 'green')
            self.can_lamp2.configure(bg = 'red')
            self.can_lamp3.configure(bg = 'red')

        if self.intvar_heater.get() == 2:
            self.can_lamp1.configure(bg = 'red')
            self.can_lamp2.configure(bg = 'green')
            self.can_lamp3.configure(bg = 'red')

        if self.intvar_heater.get() == 3 :
            self.can_lamp1.configure(bg = 'red')
            self.can_lamp2.configure(bg = 'red')
            self.can_lamp3.configure(bg = 'green')
```

```
    def off(self):
        self.can_lamp1.configure(bg = 'red')
        self.can_lamp2.configure(bg = 'red')
        self.can_lamp3.configure(bg = 'red')

root = Tk()
frontend = FrontEnd(root)

root.mainloop()
```

Prog 4 – 10

4.9 Inputting Data Using The Entry Widget

The entry widget can be used when the user needs to type in data. Prog 4 - 11 uses three entry widgets and three radio buttons to make an Ohm's law calculator. You type in the two known values in the relevant boxes and click the radio button for the unknown value, then click the "Calculate" button. There is not really much new here now. Note that the control variable option here is "textvariable". In the calc() method the ".set()" and ".get()" methods are used to get the values from the entry widgets and to write to the entry widget with the answer.


```
#prog_04_11
from Tkinter import *

class FrontEnd():
    def __init__(self, master):
        self.master = master
        self.master.title("Entry Widget Ohm's Law Calculator")

        self.doubvar_v = DoubleVar()
        self.doubvar_i = DoubleVar()
        self.doubvar_r = DoubleVar()
        self.intvar_answer = IntVar()

        self.but_calc=Button(text = 'Calculate', command = self.calc)

        self.ent_v = Entry(textvariable = self.doubvar_v)
        self.ent_i = Entry(textvariable = self.doubvar_i)
        self.ent_r = Entry(textvariable = self.doubvar_r)
```

103

```python
        self.rad_v = Radiobutton(variable = self.intvar_answer, value = 1, text = 'Volts')
        self.rad_i = Radiobutton(variable = self.intvar_answer, value = 2, text = 'Amps')
        self.rad_r=Radiobutton(variable = self.intvar_answer, value = 3, text = 'Ohms')
        self.intvar_answer.set(3)

        self.ent_v.grid(row = 0, column = 0)
        self.ent_i.grid(row = 1, column = 0)
        self.ent_r.grid(row = 2, column = 0)

        self.rad_v.grid(row = 0, column = 1)
        self.rad_i.grid(row = 1, column = 1)
        self.rad_r.grid(row = 2, column = 1)

        self.but_calc.grid(row = 0, column = 2, rowspan = 3, padx = 40, pady = 40)

    def calc(self):
        try:                                                    #To allow for unacceptable entries.
            if self.intvar_answer.get() == 1:
                self.doubvar_v.set(self.doubvar_i.get() * self.doubvar_r.get())#Note the .set() and .get().
            if self.intvar_answer.get() == 2:
                self.doubvar_i.set(self.doubvar_v.get() / self.doubvar_r.get())

            if self.intvar_answer.get() == 3:
                self.doubvar_r.set(self.doubvar_v.get() / self.doubvar_i.get())
        except:
                self.master.configure(bg = 'red')              #Warns the user garbage in!
                self.master.after(2000, self.end_alarm)        #Warning lasts 2 secons.

    def end_alarm(self):                                        #Ends warning and sets values to 0.
        self.master.configure(bg = 'grey')
        self.doubvar_v.set(0)
        self.doubvar_i.set(0)
        self.doubvar_r.set(0)

root = Tk()
frontend = FrontEnd(root)

root.mainloop()
```

Prog. 4 – 11

Something to always allow for when the user is free to type in data is, garbage in garbage out. This last program needs numerical data in, so a non numerical string will not do. Even a valid number that is accepted by the control variable can still trip you up if it results in a divide by zero error. The easy way out is the "try...except" statement that catches the problem and warns the user.

4.10 The Canvas Widget

The canvas widget has already been used to mimic indicator lamps by setting its background colour. The canvas widget is much more versatile than this, and can be drawn on while the program runs thus making animated mimics of instruments, switches and other devices. It can be used for plotting graphs. Prog 4 – 12 creates a canvas widget of 800 by 800 pixels and draws three shapes on it. The canvas is white, there is a red line, a green oval, and a blue polygon. Previously we specified colours such as red, green, grey, white, which is fine if they are the colours you want. A more flexible method is to specify the colour as three numbers; one for each primary colour, red, green and blue. Here the range for each colour is 0 to 255 decimal which is 0 to ff in hexadecimal. The colour is defined in the program as a string starting with the "#" character then two hexadecimal digits for red, then two for green and two for blue. Black is "#000000" and white is "#ffffff" , red is "#ff0000" green is "#00ff00" a darker red is "070000". This gives you 16,777,216 different choices to choose from.
You can use up to three digits per primary colour for even more choice or stay with only one digit per primary colour. The number of digits used determine what is known as colour depth.

```
#prog_04_12
from Tkinter import *

class FrontEnd():
    def __init__(self, master):
        self.master = master
        master.title("Canvas Widget")
        self.can1 = Canvas(height= 800, width = 800, bg = '#ffffff')
        self.can1.create_line(0, 0, 400, 400, fill = '#ff0000')
        self.can1.create_oval(400, 400, 800, 800, fill = '#00ff00')
        self.can1.create_polygon(0, 400, 400, 400, 400, 800, 0, 800, fill = '#0000ff')

        self.can1.grid()
```

```
root = Tk()
frontend = FrontEnd(root)
root.mainloop()
```

      Prog. 4 – 12

The coordinate system used for drawing the shapes is the Cartesian system with the origin at the top left hand corner of the canvas. The line is defined by four integers. The first is the offset to the right, the second is the offset downwards for one end of the line, the last pair of integers are the offsets for the other end of the line.

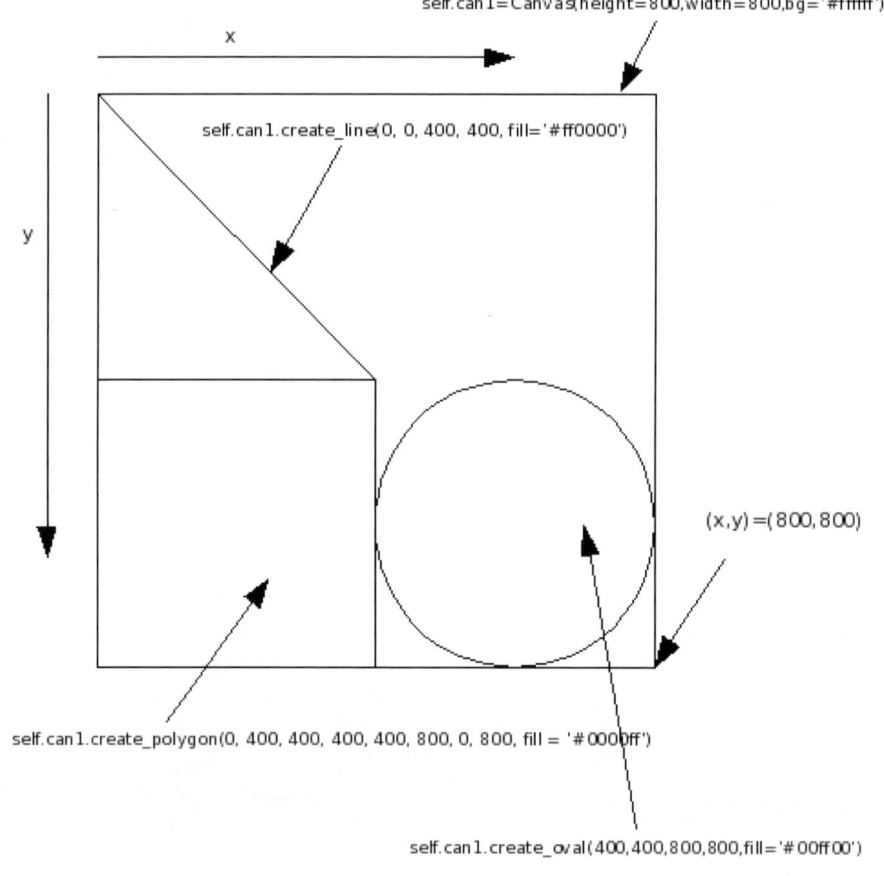

      Fig 4 – 3

106

Fig. 4 – 3 shows how the above program draws the shapes. The oval also has four integers; the first two define a corner of a rectangle, the second defines the diagonally opposite corner of the rectangle, the oval that is drawn fits this rectangle. The polygon is a succession of coordinate pairs. Three pairs draw a triangle, four pairs a rectangle and so on.

4.11 Creating an Instrument Factory

With GUIs it is possible to have mimic displays that look like the dials you find on real instrument panels. The next few programs develop a class for creating instances of an instrument with a circular dial and a moving needle. The needle's motion will be damped to give it more realism. Once the class has been written it can be used to create instruments of different diameters, ranges and graduation intervals with very little code. Fig 4 – 4 shows three mimic instruments created with the same class and displayed by one program.

When shapes are drawn on a canvas on top of one another they overlay other previously drawn shapes. The first shape drawn is a circle that is the outside of the circular dial, the next is a set of radial spokes that make up the graduation marks. The radial spokes are then overlaid with a smaller circle that leaves the outer ends of the spokes visible as graduation marks. Then the dial's numbers are added and the legend on the face. The needle and the end of the spindle are repeatedly deleted and redrawn as the interface device is read. To allow instruments of different sizes to be drawn all dimensions are expressed as proportions of the length of one side of the canvas. Therefore, whenever an instance is created only one argument for size needs to be passed to the "__init__()" method.

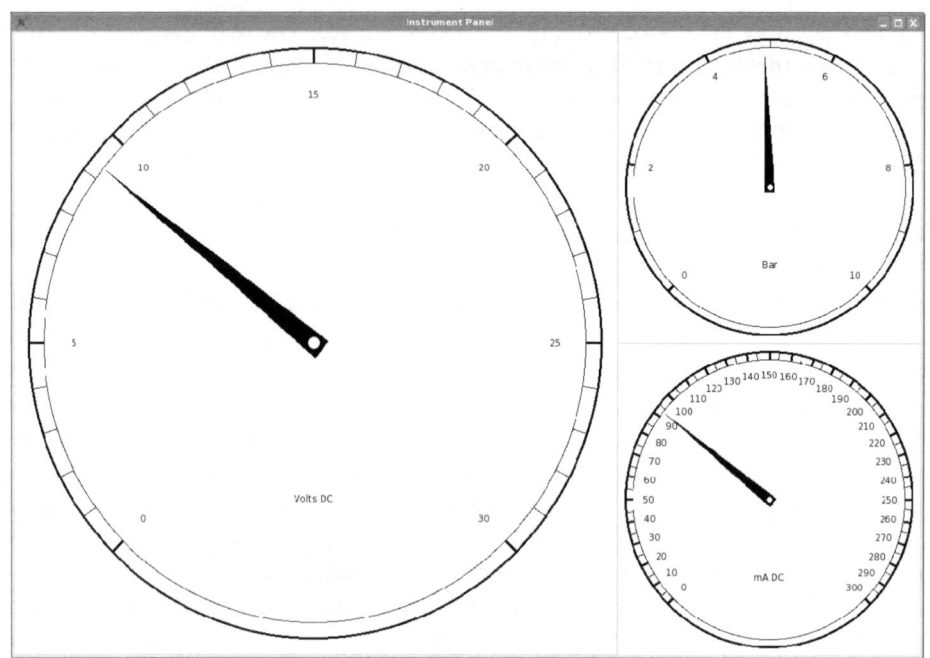

Fig. 4 – 4

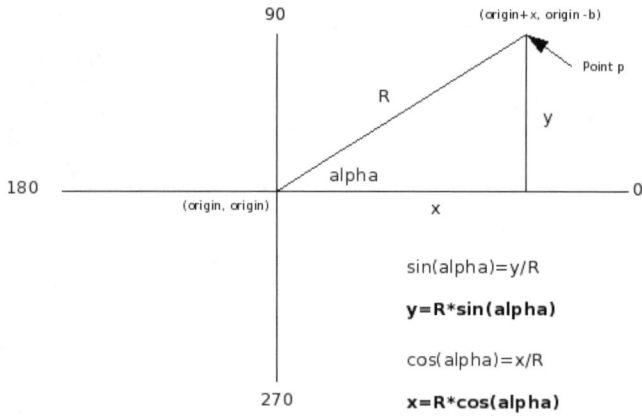

Fig. 4 – 5

Fig. 4 – 5 shows how points can be defined on the canvas in terms of an angle and a distance from an origin. First the variable "origin" is set to half the length of one side of the square canvas so the point (origin, origin) will be the centre of the canvas. The point "p" is at a distance "b" from the right of the origin and distance "a" up from the origin. To define this point in terms of the distance from the origin c and the angle alpha that c makes with the horizontal axis the trigonometric expressions on the diagram are used. Note, that because plotting on the canvas starts from the top left hand corner, moving right is positive and moving up is negative.

Prog 4 - 13 is the start of our class development. The class "Meter0()" inherits from the class Canvas. The __init__() function that runs when a new instance of a Meter is created is passed two arguments, these are the length of the side of the square canvas, and "fsd" which is the full scale deflection reading for the meter. The variable "self.R" is is the radius of the large circle, "self.r" is the radius of the small circle. The scale of our dial will have zero at angle of 225 degrees and full scale deflection at -45 degrees, an arc of 270 degrees, this can be seen by looking at Fig 4 – 4 and Fig. 4 – 5.

To plot the graduation lines we have a loop that steps from 0 to fsd. The expression "alpha_deg=(225-n*270/self.fsd)" calculates the angle to that particular spoke. The length of the spokes is "self.R" all we need now is the trigonometrical calculation to get the horizontal and vertical offsets from the origin. Imported into the program is the "math" module that contains the functions "sin()" and "cos()". These functions require the angle to be expressed in radians, and not degrees. If you are not familiar with radians, an angle of one radian is the angle that a line fixed at one end would rotate through if the other end moved in a plane a distance equal to its length. As the circumference of a circle is 2 multiplied by pi multiplied by the radius there are 2 times pi radians in 360 degrees. Python makes this very easy as there are two functions available in the math module to do this conversion; "radians()" to get radians from degrees and degrees() to get degrees from radians.

```
#prog_04_13
from Tkinter import *
from math import *

class Meter0(Canvas):
    def __init__(self, side, fsd):
        self.side = side
        self.fsd = fsd
        self.orig = self.side/2.0
        self.R = 0.95*self.side/2
```

```
      self.r = 0.9*self.side/2
      self.num_r = 0.8*self.side/2
      self.can_meter = Canvas(height = self.side, width = self.side, bg = '#707070')
      self.can_meter.create_oval(self.orig - self.R, self.orig - self.R, self.orig + \
      self.R, self.orig + self.R, fill = '#ffffff', width = 3)
      for n in range (0, self.fsd + 1):
         alpha_deg = (225 - n * 270/self.fsd)
         alpha = radians(alpha_deg)
         y = self.R * sin(alpha)
         x = self.R * cos(alpha)
         self.can_meter.create_line(self.orig, self.orig, self.orig + x, self.orig - y)

class FrontEnd():
   def __init__(self, master):
      self.master = master
      master.title("Instrument Panel")
      self.meter1 = Meter0(800, 30)
      self.meter1.can_meter.grid(row = 0, column = 0, rowspan = 2)

root = Tk()
frontend = FrontEnd(root)
root.mainloop()
```

Prog. 4 – 13

So far we have plotted a graduation line at every integer between 0 and fsd. What we are going to produce are major graduation marks with numbers next to them and minor graduation marks between them. The intervals between these lines will be set by arguments passed to the "__init__()" method. Prog 4 – 14 adds two "if" statements to decide if to plot a major or minor mark or not, and to make the major marks red. A circle of radius "self.r" is then drawn to cover over the spokes leaving the ends visible.

```
#prog_04_14

from Tkinter import *
from math import *

class Meter0(Canvas):
   def __init__(self, side, fsd, grad_maj, grad_min):
      self.side = side
      self.fsd = fsd
      self.grad_maj = grad_maj
```

```python
        self.grad_min = grad_min
        self.orig = self.side/2.0
        self.R = 0.95*self.side/2
        self.r = 0.9*self.side/2
        self.num_r = 0.8 * self.side/2
        self.can_meter = Canvas(height = self.side,width = self.side, bg = '#707070')
        self.can_meter.create_oval(self.orig - self.R, self.orig - self.R,\
        self.orig + self.R, self.orig + self.R, fill = '#ffffff', width = 3)
        for n in range (0, self.fsd + 1):
            alpha_deg = (225 - n * 270/self.fsd)
            alpha = radians(alpha_deg)

            if n%self.grad_min == 0:
                y = self.R * sin(alpha)
                x = self.R * cos(alpha)
                self.can_meter.create_line(self.orig, self.orig, self.orig + x, self.orig - y)
            if n%self.grad_maj == 0:
                y = self.R*sin(alpha)
                x = self.R*cos(alpha)
                self.can_meter.create_line(self.orig, self.orig,\
                self.orig + x, self.orig - y, fill= '#ff0000', width = 3)

        self.can_meter.create_oval(self.orig - self.r, self.orig - self.r, self.orig + \
        self.r, self.orig + self.r)

class FrontEnd():
    def __init__(self,master):
        self.master = master
        master.title("Instrument Panel")
        self.meter1 = Meter0(800,30,5,1)
        self.meter1.can_meter.grid(row = 0, column = 0, rowspan = 2)

root = Tk()
frontend = FrontEnd(root)
root.mainloop()
```

Prog. 4 – 14

To put text on a canvas there is "create_text()" method. The options we are using here are the horizontal and vertical offsets and the string for the text to be printed. The same trigonometrical technique is used here as before with a new variable "num_r" that sets the distance from the origin for the text. One further argument has been passed to the "__init__()" method, that is the legend to be printed on the instrument face.

111

```
#prog_04_15

from Tkinter import *
from math import *

class Meter0(Canvas):
    def __init__(self, side, fsd, grad_maj, grad_min, units):
        self.side = side
        self.fsd = fsd
        self.grad_maj = grad_maj
        self.grad_min = grad_min
        self.units = units
        self.orig = self.side/2.0
        self.R = 0.95*self.side/2
        self.r = 0.9*self.side/2
        self.num_r = 0.8 * self.side/2
        self.can_meter = Canvas(height = self.side, width = self.side, bg = '#707070')
        self.can_meter.create_oval(self.orig - self.R, self.orig - self.R, self.orig +\
        self.R, self.orig + self.R, fill = '#ffffff', width = 3)
        for n in range (0, self.fsd + 1):
            alpha_deg = (225 - n * 270/self.fsd)
            alpha = radians(alpha_deg)
            if n%self.grad_min == 0:
                y = self.R * sin(alpha)
                x = self.R * cos(alpha)
                self.can_meter.create_line(self.orig,self.orig,self.orig+x,self.orig - y)
            if n%self.grad_maj == 0:
                y = self.R * sin(alpha)
                x = self.R*cos(alpha)
                self.can_meter.create_line(self.orig,self.orig,self.orig + x, self.orig - y,\
                fill = '#ff0000', width = 3)

        self.can_meter.create_oval(self.orig - self.r, self.orig - self.r,\
        self.orig + self.r, self.orig + self.r, fill = '#ffffff')

        for n in range (0, self.fsd + 1):
            alpha_deg = (225 - n * 270.0/self.fsd)
            alpha = radians(alpha_deg)
            if n%self.grad_maj == 0:
                y = self.num_r * sin(alpha)
                x = self.num_r * cos(alpha)
                self.can_meter.create_text(self.orig + x,self.orig - y, \
                text=str(n), fill = '#ffffff')
```

self.can_meter.create_text(self.orig,self.orig*1.5,text = self.units,fill = '#ffffff')

```
class FrontEnd():
    def __init__(self,master):
        self.master = master
        master.title("Instrument Panel")
        self.meter1 = Meter0(800,30,5,1,'Volts DC')
        self.meter1.can_meter.grid(row = 0, column = 0, rowspan = 2)

root=Tk()
frontend = FrontEnd(root)
root.mainloop()
```

Prog. 4 – 15

"Note that a separate loop has been used for the numbers as they have to go on top of the smaller circle.

So far we have created the basic dial and now it needs a function to read the FTDI device and draw a needle pointing to the correct reading. Prog 4 – 16 adds this function, but first an explanation as to how the needle is constructed. Fig. 4 – 6 shows that the needle is a triangle "abc". The angle alpha is calculated from the value read from the interface device, point b is at a distance 0.025 times the length of the side of the canvas and at an angle of alpha plus 135 degrees. Point a is the same but at an angle of alpha minus 135 degrees.

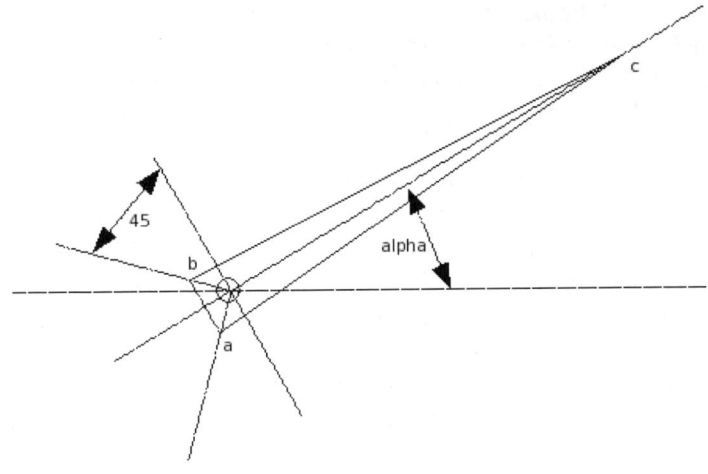

Fig. 4 – 6

113

```
#prog_04_16

from Tkinter import *
from math import *
import _simple_ftdi

class Meter0(Canvas):
    handle = 0
    def __init__(self, side, fsd, grad_maj, grad_min, units, serial):
        self.handle = Meter0.handle
        Meter0.handle = Meter0.handle + 1
        self.side = side
        self.fsd = fsd
        self.grad_maj = grad_maj
        self.grad_min = grad_min
        self.units = units
        self.serial = serial
        self.reading = 0
        self.orig = self.side/2.0
        self.R = 0.95*self.side/2
        self.r = 0.9*self.side/2
        self.num_r = 0.8*self.side/2
        self.can_meter = Canvas(height = self.side, width = self.side, bg = '#707070')
        self.can_meter.create_oval(self.orig - self.R, self.orig - self.R,\
        self.orig + self.R, self.orig + self.R, fill = '#ffffff', width = 3)
        for n in range (0, self.fsd + 1):
            alpha_deg = (225 - n * 270/self.fsd)
            alpha = radians(alpha_deg)
            if n%self.grad_min == 0:
                y = self.R * sin(alpha)
                x = self.R * cos(alpha)
                self.can_meter.create_line(self.orig, self.orig, self.orig + x, self.orig - y)
            if n%self.grad_maj == 0:
                y = self.R * sin(alpha)
                x = self.R * cos(alpha)
                self.can_meter.create_line(self.orig, self.orig, self.orig + x, self.orig - y, \
                fill = '#ff0000', width = 3)

        self.can_meter.create_oval(self.orig - self.r, self.orig-self.r,\
        self.orig + self.r, self.orig + self.r, fill = '#ffffff')

        for n in range (0,self.fsd+1):
            alpha_deg=(225 - n*270.0/self.fsd)
            alpha=radians(alpha_deg)
```

114

```python
        if n%self.grad_maj==0:
            y=self.num_r*sin(alpha)
            x=self.num_r*cos(alpha)
            self.can_meter.create_text(self.orig + x,self.orig - y, text=str(n))

    self.can_meter.create_text(self.orig,self.orig*1.5,text=self.units)

def read(self):
        try:
            self.can_meter.delete(self.spindle)
            self.can_meter.delete(self.needle)
        except:
            pass
        self.device_up=_simple_ftdi.open_device(self.serial,self.handle,0)
        if self.device_up == 0:
            self.reading_r = _simple_ftdi.read_pins(self.handle)
            _simple_ftdi.close_device(self.handle)
        else:
            self.reading_r = -20

        self.reading = self.reading+(self.reading_r-self.reading)/5.0    #Needle damping
        alpha_deg = (225 - self.reading * 270.0/255)
        alpha = radians(alpha_deg)
        beta = radians(135)
        ax = self.orig+0.025 * self.side * cos(alpha - beta)
        ay = self.orig - 0.025 * self.side * sin(alpha - beta)
        bx = self.orig + 0.025 * self.side * cos(alpha + beta)
        by = self.orig - 0.025 * self.side * sin(alpha + beta)
        cx = self.orig + self.r * cos(alpha)
        cy = self.orig - self.r * sin(alpha)
        self.needle = self.can_meter.create_polygon(ax, ay, bx, by, cx, cy)
        self.spindle = self.can_meter.create_oval(self.orig - 0.01 * self.side, \
        self.orig - 0.01 * self.side, self.orig + 0.01 * self.side, self.orig +0.01 \
        * self.side, fill = '#ffffff')

class FrontEnd():
    def __init__(self,master):
        self.master = master
        master.title("Instrument Panel")
        self.meter1 = Meter0(800,30,5,1,'Volts DC','FTCVIMKA')
        self.meter1.can_meter.grid(row = 0, column = 0, rowspan = 2)
        self.inputs()

    def inputs(self):
```

115

```
        self.meter1.read()
        self.master.after(2,self.inputs)

root = Tk()
frontend = FrontEnd(root)
root.mainloop()
```

Prog. 4 – 16

Prog 4 – 16 is the final operating instrument class. Another argument has been added to the
"__init__()" method, this is the serial number of the device that is driving that instance.
The module "_simple_ftdi" has to be imported. In order for the meter to read the method
".read()" for that instance has to be called, this is done by the "inputs()" method in
FrontEnd(), "inputs()" is called repeatedly by the ".after()" method. The needle damping is
achieved by not moving the meter to the correct value instantaneously but by moving it
only a proportion of the difference between the true reading and the last reading, this way
the needle progressively slows as it approaches the correct reading, by the line
"self.reading=self.reading+(self.reading_r – self.reading)/5.0". The user is alerted to a
missing device by the needle being driven below zero, a missing device returns -1 from
"_simple_ftdi".

Now that the class Meter0() is finished to make things more convenient the class is saved
in file named "instruments.py" which can be used by importing it as in Prog 4 – 17.

```
#prog_04_17
from Tkinter import *
from instruments import *

class FrontEnd():
    def __init__(self, master):
        self.master = master
        master.title("Instrument Panel")
        self.meter1 = Meter0(600, 30, 5, 1, 'Volts DC', 'FTCVIMKA')
        self.meter2 = Meter0(400, 30 ,5 ,1, 'Volts DC', 'FTCVIMKA')

        self.meter1.can_meter.grid(row = 0, column = 0)
        self.meter2.can_meter.grid(row = 0, column = 2)

        self.inputs()
```

```
    def inputs(self):
        self.meter1.read()
        self.meter2.read()
        self.master.after(2,self.inputs)

root = Tk()
frontend = FrontEnd(root)
root.mainloop()
```

Prog 4 – 17

To create more instruments is just a matter of adding more instances, as in Prog 4 – 18

```
#prog_04_18
from Tkinter import *
from instruments import *

class FrontEnd():
    def __init__(self, master):
        self.master = master
        master.title("Instrument Panel")
        self.meter1 = Meter0(800, 3000, 100, 10, 'RPM', 'FTCVIMKA')
        self.meter2 = Meter0(400, 100, 10, 1, 'Degrees C','FTCVMOYU')
        self.meter3 = Meter0(400,30,10,2,'Volts DC','FTCVIMKA')
        self.meter1.can_meter.grid(row = 0, column = 0, rowspan = 2)
        self.meter2.can_meter.grid(row = 0, column = 1, rowspan = 1)
        self.meter3.can_meter.grid(row = 1, column = 1, rowspan = 1)

        self.inputs()

    def inputs(self):
        self.meter1.read()
        self.meter2.read()
        self.meter3.read()
        self.master.after(2, self.inputs)

root = Tk()
frontend = FrontEnd(root)
root.mainloop()
```

Prog 4 – 18

117

4.12 Binding Events

You are not restricted to clicking on buttons to make things happen. You can use all sorts of events like moving the mouse, or pressing a particular key to call a method. This is done by binding the event you want to use to the method you want to call. We will modify one of the earlier programs so that rolling the mouse over the indicator lamps switches the heater. In Prog. 4 – 19 which is similar to Prog 4 – 3 the buttons have been removed and two new lines added which use the ".bind()" method. This method binds the action of moving the mouse over the widget by the string "<Motion>" to the method self.switch() that has replaced the "on()" and "off()" methods. The bind method passes an object "event" to the method "self.switch()". This object has an attribute .widget which is the widget that is associated with the mouse move event. The "if" statements decide if the heater is to be switched on or off.

```
#prog_04_19

from Tkinter import *

class FrontEnd():
    def __init__(self,master):
        self.master=master
        self.master.title('Heater Controller')
        self.can_on_lamp = Canvas(width = 40, height = 40, bg = 'grey')
        self.can_off_lamp = Canvas(width = 40, height = 40, bg = 'red')
        self.lab_heater_on = Label(text = 'ON')
        self.lab_heater_off = Label(text = 'OFF')

        self.can_off_lamp.bind('<Motion>', self.switch)      #.bind() method binds the moving of
                                                             #the mouse over the canvas
        self.can_on_lamp.bind('<Motion>', self.switch)       #to the self.switch method

        self.lab_heater_off.grid(row = 0, column = 0)
        self.lab_heater_on.grid(row = 0, column = 1)
        self.can_off_lamp.grid(row = 1, column = 0, padx = 10, pady = 10)
        self.can_on_lamp.grid(row = 1, column = 1, padx = 10 ,pady = 10)

    def switch(self,event):
        if event.widget == self.can_on_lamp:
            self.can_on_lamp.configure(bg = 'green')
            self.can_off_lamp.configure(bg = 'grey')
```

```
    if event.widget == self.can_off_lamp:
        self.can_on_lamp.configure(bg = 'grey')
        self.can_off_lamp.configure(bg = 'red')

root = Tk()
frontend = FrontEnd(root)
root.mainloop()
```

Prog 4 – 19

Chapter 5

Bit Map Graphics

5.1 Introduction

This chapter is mainly about the anatomy of bit map images and how to operate on them. In the last chapter the canvas widget was used to draw on when producing GUIs in Tkinter. What if you want to plot a graph and save it as an image file? Python does provide a method for saving canvases as postscript files, but what we will do in this chapter is create and modify bitmap images that can be used both for saving graphics and for transmitting them over networks. Bit map images are very easy to manipulate as they are an array of pixels like points on a piece of graph paper.

5.2 The Bit Map File

The bit map images we will be dealing with will have each pixel colour defined by three bytes, one for each primary colour. As an illustration Fig 5 – 1 represents an image using 8 by 6 pixels. There is a square for each pixel and a byte for each of the three colours. The image is white except for a red line across the top and the three pixels starting from the bottom left hand corner are red, green and blue.

B = 0 G = 0 R = 255	B = 0 G = 0 R = 255	B = 0 G = 0 R = 255	B = 0 G = 0 R = 255	B = 0 G = 0 R = 255	B = 0 G = 0 R = 255	B = 0 G = 0 R = 255	B = 0 G = 0 R = 255	–RED LINE
B = 255 G = 255 R = 255	B = 255 G = 255 R = 255	B = 255 G = 255 R = 255	B = 255 G = 255 R = 255	B = 255 G = 255 R = 255	B = 255 G = 255 R = 255	B = 255 G = 255 R = 255	B = 255 G = 255 R = 255	
B = 255 G = 255 R = 255	B = 255 G = 255 R = 255	B = 255 G = 255 R = 255	B = 255 G = 255 R = 255	B = 255 G = 255 R = 255	B = 255 G = 255 R = 255	B = 255 G = 255 R = 255	B = 255 G = 255 R = 255	
B = 255 G = 255 R = 255	B = 255 G = 255 R = 255	B = 255 G = 255 R = 255	B = 255 G = 255 R = 255	B = 255 G = 255 R = 255	B = 255 G = 255 R = 255	B = 255 G = 255 R = 255	B = 255 G = 255 R = 255	
B = 255 G = 255 R = 255	B = 255 G = 255 R = 255	B = 255 G = 255 R = 255	B = 255 G = 255 R = 255	B = 255 G = 255 R = 255	B = 255 G = 255 R = 255	B = 255 G = 255 R = 255	B = 255 G = 255 R = 255	
B = 0 G = 0 R = 255	B = 0 G = 255 R = 0	B = 255 G = 0 R = 0	B = 255 G = 255 R = 255	B = 255 G = 255 R = 255	B = 255 G = 255 R = 255	B = 255 G = 255 R = 255	B = 255 G = 255 R = 255	

RED   GREEN   BLUE   PIXELS

Fig. 5 - 1

Not shown on Fig 5 – 1 the bit map file starts with a string of 54 bytes called the 'header'. The header contains information about the image, but we needn't worry about the content of the header for now. Following the header is the actual image content; starting from the bottom left hand corner of the image the next three bytes are the blue, green, then red values of the first pixel. This continues for each pixel in the bottom row. After the bottom row begins the left most pixel of the next row up and then so on for the rest of the image. There is an application on the CD called "KolourPaint". This is adequate for viewing and modifying our images. Fig 5 – 1 is on the CD its name is "fig1image.bmp". To view it you will need maximum zoom.

Fig 5 – 2 shows how the bytes that define the image are sequenced in the file. The first four pixels and the last two from Fig 5 – 1. Note that the order of the bytes for each pixel is blue, green and then red.

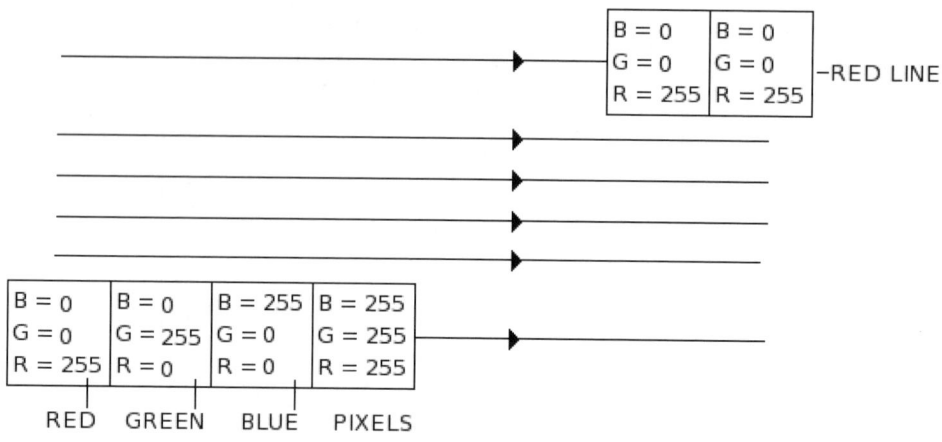

RED   GREEN   BLUE   PIXELS

HEADER   IMAGE CONTENT

Fig. 5 – 2

The object of the exercise is to write an image file with our own program. This will be referred to as the output file. Although we don't need to worry about the content of the header we do need a header for any file we create. Fortunately, the header does not depend on the image content but only on the geometry of the image and the colour depth. The easiest way to write the header for your file is to copy the header from another image of the same size and colour depth. We will look at the make up of the header later in this chapter.

We will take an existing bit map file, our template image, and read it. The header will be re-used as the header of the output file. The template file can give the program a head start by having a background such as the grid lines for a graph or the face of an instrument to draw on top of.

Looking again at Fig 5 – 1 each square is a pixel and needs three bytes to set its colour. We can create a list with three members each being an integer from 0 to 255; this would mean the third pixel from the left hand corner would be [255, 0, 0]. If we have a separate list for

122

each pixel we need some way of identifying these lists in terms of where they are on the image. One Python object that is ideal for this is the dictionary. Dictionaries were covered in chapter 2. The members of a dictionary are indexed by keys. See below how any pixel from Fig 5 – 1 could be held in a dictionary. The keys that we are going to use to index the lists that define the pixel colours are tuples with two integer members. These integers are the horizontal and vertical offsets from the bottom left hand corner of the image.

image_content_dictionary = {(0, 0) : [0, 0, 255] , (7, 2) : [255, 255, 255], (7, 5) : [0, 0, 255].................}

To change the colour of any pixel, for example the top left hand corner, which is x offset 0 and y offset 5 to a dark blue, you would use:

image_content_dictionary[(0,5)]= [127, 0, 0]

5.3 The Struct Module

When we read the template file what we will have is one long string of bytes. Python will treat this as a long text string which is not what we want. Files are just strings of bytes. If it is a text file a text editor will read the bytes which are just numbers and convert them to printable characters or if they are control codes it will implement them.

A bit map image is not meant to be interpreted as a text file; the bytes in the image content mean colours. We want each byte after the header to be converted to an integer, then grouped in lists of three, each list being a pixel and each list stored in a dictionary where its key defines its coordinates in the image. Python provides a module called 'struct' that can take bytes from a string and convert them to a number. It can also take numbers and form strings with them.

The two methods to look at are pack() and unpack(). To make the following demonstration simpler to carry out I will choose two byte values that are printable characters 'd' which has the ASCII value 100 and 'A' which is 65.
The unpack() method is used like this:

number = struct.unpack('B', 'd').

This will take the single byte string 'd' and convert it to an integer. The significance of the 'B' is to tell unpack() that it wants one byte and it is unsigned.   Trying this at the interactive Python prompt:

```
>>> from struct import *
>>> number = unpack('B' , 'd')
>>> print number
(100,)
>>>
```

The answer is a tuple whose member is the integer 100. This is as complicated as it needs to get for dealing with single bytes. However to give you an idea what else can be done I will show a couple of other things. One byte can only represent 256 different values and two bytes can represent 65536 different values. Suppose we take the two byte string 'dA' this can be looked as either the 'd' is the high order byte or the 'A' is the high order byte. The two possible unsigned answers are as:

100*256 + 65 =25665

or

65*256+100 = 16740.

To do this with unpack the two options are:

number =unpack('>H','dA')
and

number =unpack('<H','dA')
The 'H' means that it is unpacking a word.

```
>>> number=unpack('>H', 'dA')
>>> print number
(25665,)
>>>
```

```
>>> number=unpack('<H','dA')
>>> print number
(16740,)
>>>
```

Three bytes could be unpacked like this, a word and a single byte. The number of bytes available to unpack must match the formatting.

```
>>> numbers = unpack('>HB', 'dAd')
>>> print numbers
(25665, 100)
>>>
```

The pack() method works the same way but in reverse.

```
>>> string = pack('>HB', 25665, 100)
>>> print string
dAd
```

5.4 The Image

Prog 5 – 1 takes the bitmap file for Fig 5 – 1 and prints out a dictionary with all the image content. This is a too small an image to be of any practical use but it allows us to see the entire dictionary.

```
#prog_05_01.py

from struct import *

X = 8                                          #8 pixels wide.
Y = 6                                          #6 pixels high.
template_file=open("fig1_image.bmp", 'r')      #Opens template file to read.
file_string = template_file.read()             #Reads entire file into a string.
template_file.close()                          #Close file.
header_string = file_string[0:54]              #Slice off the header.
bit_map_string = file_string[54:]              #Slice off the image content.
bit_map_dict = {}                              #Create empty dictionary.

for y in range (0, Y):                         #Vertical offsets loop.
  for x in range (0, X):                       #Horizontal offsets loop.
    key=(x, y)                                 #Generates key for each pixel.
    pixel_colour_list=[]                       #Empty list for each pixel.
    for c in range (0, 3):                     #Steps through each byte for each pixel.
      t = unpack('B', bit_map_string[3 * (y * X + x ) + c])     #Unpacks the byte for
                                                                #that colour and pixel.

      pixel_colour_list.append(t[0])           #Appends the integer  to the pixel's list note
                                               #it is a tuple hence t[0].
```

125

```
            bit_map_dict[key] = pixel_colour_list        #Creates an entry in the dictionary.

print bit_map_dict                                       #Prints out the dictionary.
```

Prog. 5 – 1

Below is the dictionary printed out, note Python orders the dictionary to suit itself.

root@slax:~# python prog_05_01.py
{(7, 3): [255, 255, 255], (1, 3): [255, 255, 255], (3, 0): [255, 255, 255], (5, 4): [255, 255, 255], (2, 1): [255, 255, 255], (6, 2): [255, 255, 255], (5, 1): [255, 255, 255], (0, 3): [255, 255, 255], (2, 5): [0, 0, 255], (7, 2): [255, 255, 255], (4, 0): [255, 255, 255], (1, 2): [255, 255, 255], (3, 3): [255, 255, 255], (4, 4): [255, 255, 255], (6, 3): [255, 255, 255], (1, 5): [0, 0, 255], (5, 0): [255, 255, 255], (2, 2): [255, 255, 255], (3, 5): [0, 0, 255], (4, 1): [255, 255, 255], (1, 1): [255, 255, 255], (6, 4): [255, 255, 255], (3, 2): [255, 255, 255], (0, 0): [0, 0, 255], (7, 1): [255, 255, 255], (4, 5): [0, 0, 255], (0, 4): [255, 255, 255], (6, 0): [255, 255, 255], (1, 4): [255, 255, 255], (5, 5): [0, 0, 255], (7, 5): [0, 0, 255], (2, 3): [255, 255, 255], (4, 2): [255, 255, 255], (1, 0): [0, 255, 0], (6, 5): [0, 0, 255], (5, 3): [255, 255, 255], (0, 1): [255, 255, 255], (7, 0): [255, 255, 255], (3, 4): [255, 255, 255], (6, 1): [255, 255, 255], (3, 1): [255, 255, 255], (2, 4): [255, 255, 255], (7, 4): [255, 255, 255], (2, 0): [255, 0, 0], (4, 3): [255, 255, 255], (0, 5): [0, 0, 255], (5, 2): [255, 255, 255], (0, 2): [255, 255, 255]}
root@slax:~#

In Prog 5 – 1 are three nested loops, the outer two loops step through every pixel, every permutation of x and y is a pixel in the image and the tuple (x, y) is the key to that pixel_colour_list in the dictionary.

In the inner loop is an awkward looking expression "t=unpack('B', bit_map_string[3*(y*X+x)+c])". The inner loop steps through the three bytes for that pixel and unpacks each to a tuple containing one integer. This integer is appended to the pixel_colour_list for that pixel. The expression $3*(y*X+x)+c$ indexes to the byte we want to unpack. Fig 5 – 2 shows how the first 36 bytes of the 8 pixel wide image are ordered in the file and how by using the y the x and the c offsets you can access the colour byte you want.

126

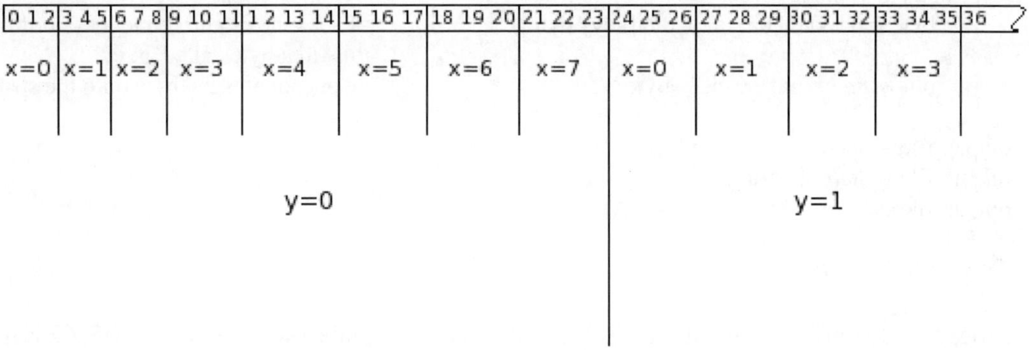

0 1 2	3 4 5	6 7 8	9 10 11	12 13 14	15 16 17	18 19 20	21 22 23	24 25 26	27 28 29	30 31 32	33 34 35	36
x=0	x=1	x=2	x=3	x=4	x=5	x=6	x=7	x=0	x=1	x=2	x=3	

y=0   y=1

Fig. 5 – 2

```
#prog_05_02.py

from struct import *

X = 800
Y = 600
template_file = open("template_05_02.bmp",'r')
bit_map_string = template_file.read()
template_file.close()
header_string = bit_map_string[0:54]
bit_map_string = bit_map_string[54:]
bit_map_dict = {}

for y in range (0, Y):
    for x in range (0, X):
        key = (x, y)
        pixel_list = []
        for c in range (0, 3):
            t = unpack('B',bit_map_string[3 * (y * X + x) + c])
            pixel_list.append(t[0])
            bit_map_dict[key] = pixel_list

out_string = header_string                    #Starts the output string with the header.

for y in range (0,Y):
    for x in range (0,X):
        key = (x,y)
```

```
    for byte in range (0, 3):
        byte = pack('B',bit_map_dict[key][byte])        #Packs the required integer out of the
                                                         #list to a byte called 'byte'.

        out_string = out_string + byte                   #Concatinates the byte onto the string.

output_file = open("output.bmp", 'w')
output_file.write(out_string)
output_file.close()
```

Prog. 5 – 2

Prog. 5 – 2 is going to handle an 800 x 600 pixel template file " template_05_02.bmp", which, if you look at it, is the background for a graph. What has been added here is more code to write a bit map file that is a copy of the template file. Dealing with the new code; first the sliced off header is used as the start of the string that will be the output file. Then there are three nested loops where the outer two, step through the image in correct pixel order to create a key that will access the pixel colour list from the dictionary. The inner loop steps through the members of that pixel's colour list and packs a byte for that value. The byte is then concatenated onto the 'out_string'. Then finally the 'output.bmp' is opened for writing and the 'out_string' written to it. Now we have an exact copy of the template file called 'output.bmp'. That was a lot of work to copy a file! The point is that part way through the process we have a dictionary that is easy to use to modify the image content as the next program will demonstrate.

5.5 A New Image

```
#prog_05_03.py

from struct import *
from math import  sin, radians          #You don't need to import everything

X = 800
Y = 600
template_file = open("template_05_02.bmp", 'r')
bit_map_string = template_file.read()
template_file.close()
header_string = bit_map_string[0:54]
bit_map_string = bit_map_string[54:]
bit_map_dict = {}
```

128

```
for y in range (0, Y):
    for x in range (0, X):
        key=(x, y)
        pixel_list = []
        for c in range (0, 3):
            t = unpack('B', bit_map_string[3 * (y * X + x) + c])
            pixel_list.append(t[0])
            bit_map_dict[key] = pixel_list

for x in range(0, X):
    x_rad = radians(x * 360.0/X)
    y = int(0.5*Y + 0.5*Y*sin(x_rad))
    bit_map_dict[(x, y)] = [0,0,255]

out_string = header_string

for y in range (0, Y):
    for x in range (0, X):
        key=(x, y)
        for c in range (0, 3):
            byte=pack('B', bit_map_dict[key][c])
            out_string=out_string + byte

output_file = open("output.bmp", 'w')
output_file.write(out_string)
output_file.close()
```

Prog. 5 – 3

What has been added is a loop that plots a sine wave that fits one cycle onto the graph. The important point here is that we can alter any pixel on the image by using the dictionary to change the colour of that pixel. The sine wave is plotted in red. For all the values of x, the value y=sin(x) is calculated, scaled and offset to fit the image. Where a red dot is to be plotted the dictionary member for that pixel is set to [0,0,255] which is red. This way you draw on top of anything that is already there.

5.6 The Header

The code is starting to get messy. It is fine for a demonstration but it would be better if it was bundled up in a class in a separate module and imported when needed. Also having to set the size of the image explicitly in the program is inconvenient. At the start of the chapter it was said that the header contained information about the image. So now is the time to look at the bytes that make up the header. The header is actually comprised of two parts, the first part is called the header file and is the first 14 bytes, the remainder is the header information and is in our case 40 bytes. Table 5 – 1 describes the meaning of the bytes in the header. Some of the information takes two bytes and some four bytes. Taking the bytes in the order they are read, the first byte is the low order byte. The variable names given in the table are not official names; they are the names used in Prog 5 – 4 to read a real header.

Byte	Variable	Purpose	Byte	Variable	Purpose
0	type_	The type of file for a bit map file the two bytes are ASCII for 'BM'	26	planes	Always 1
1			27		
2	size	The size of the file in bytes	28	depth	The colour depth. For us it will always be 24.
3			29		
4			30	compression	For us it will be 0. No compression
5			31		
6	reserved	Not used	32		
7			33		
8			34	image_length	The length of the image content. For us it will always be 3 times width times height. See information on 'junk' bytes.
9			35		
10	offset	The offset of the start of the image content. For us it will be 54	36		
11			37		
12			38	x_metre	Pixels per metre in the horizontal direction, only relevent for printers.
13			39		
14	info_size	The size of the header info. For us it will be 50	40		
15			41		
16			42	y_metre	Pixels per metre in the
17			43		

130

18	width	The width of the image in pixels.	44		vertical direction, only relevent for printers.
19			45		
20			46	col_used	Default is 0 meaning 2**n colours used.
21			47		
22	height	The height of the image in pixels	48		
23			49		
24			50	col_sig	Number of important colours default is 0 meaning all colours.
25			51		
			52		
			53		

Table 5 – 1

Prog 5 – 4 reads and prints out the information from headers in bit map files

```
#prog_05_04.py

from struct import *

X = 800
Y = 600
template_file = open("template_05_02.bmp", 'r')
bit_map_string = template_file.read()
template_file.close()
header_string = bit_map_string[0:54]
type_ = header_string[0:2]
size  = unpack('I', header_string[2:6])
reserved1 = unpack('I', header_string[6:10])
offset = unpack('I', header_string[10:14])
info_size = unpack('I', header_string[14:18])
width = unpack('I', header_string[18:22])
height = unpack('I', header_string[22:26])
planes = unpack('H', header_string[26:28])
depth = unpack('H', header_string[28:30])
compression = unpack('I', header_string[30:34])
image_length = unpack('I', header_string[34:38])
```

131

```
x_metre = unpack('I', header_string[38:42])
y_metre = unpack('I', header_string[42:46])
col_used = unpack('I', header_string[46:50])
col_sig = unpack('I', header_string[50:54])
print 'type = ' + type_
print 'size  =' + str(size[0])
print 'reserved1 = ' + str(reserved1[0])
print 'offset = ' + str(offset[0])
print 'width = ' + str(width[0])
print 'height = ' + str(height[0])
print 'planes = ' + str(planes[0])
print 'depth = ' + str(depth[0])
print 'compression = ' + str(compression[0])
print 'image_length = ' + str(image_length[0])
print 'x_metre = ' + str(x_metre[0])
print 'y_metre = ' + str(y_metre[0])
print 'col_used = ' + str(col_used[0])
print 'col_sig = ' + str(col_sig[0])
```

Prog. 5 – 4

Running Prog 5 - 4 gives the following.

```
root@slax:~# python prog_05_04.py
type = BM
size  =1440054
reserved1=0
offset=54
width=800
height=600
planes=1
depth=24
compression=0
image_length=1440000
x_metre=2834                    #72 dots per inch
y_metre=2834
col_used=0
col_sig=0
root@slax:~#
```

The width and the height are two useful pieces of information that can be extracted from the header.

5.7 Junk Bytes

Up until now, the number of pixels in the horizontal direction have been divisible by four, to keep it simple but all the images we will use will be like this. The reason for this is that the bit map format requires the number of bytes in a row of pixels to be divisible by four, if it is not then extra bytes are added on the end of each row to pad out the total. For example if you had an image that was 15 pixels wide then that would have 45 bytes per row, but 45 divided by four leaves one remainder. So in order to conform 3 bytes would be added to make the number 48. This would make our program a bit more complicated. The easiest way round it is to avoid widths that do not divide by four! To demonstrate this, 'junk_bytes.bmp' is an image that is 103 pixels wide by 100 pixels high. If there were no need for padding it would have 103 times 3 times 100 plus 54 bytes which is 30954. As a row of 103 pixels has 309 bytes which leaves one left over when divided by four it gets padded to 312 bytes per row.
The extra 3 bytes per row give 300 extra for the whole image as it 100 high. Long listing this file gives 31254 which shows there are 300 extra bytes.

```
root@slax:~# ls -l junk_bytes.bmp
-rw-r--r-- 1 root root 31254 Nov  5 19:45 junk_bytes.bmp
root@slax:~#
```

5.8 Class BmpDraw

The next step is to develop a class that can be re-used by programs by just importing. Prog 5 – 5 is the start of this class, it checks to see if it is a bitmap file, then obtains values for the width and the height of the image. The program can be run to produce a sine wave overlaid on the template file because of the extra code at the bottom of the file that starts with "if __name__ == '__main__':". This code will not run if the file is imported into another program but is there so that the file can be used as a stand alone program.

```python
#prog_05_05.py

from struct import *
from math import  *

class BmpDraw:
    def __init__(self, infile_name):
        try:
            template_file = open(infile_name, 'r')
```

```
        bit_map_string=template_file.read()
        template_file.close()
    except:
        self.flag = -1
        print 'Failed no template file!'
        return

    if bit_map_string[0:2] != 'BM':
        self.flag = -1
        print 'Failed not a .bmp!'
        return

    self.flag = 1
    self.header_string = bit_map_string[0:54]
    self.image_content_string = bit_map_string[54:]
    width = unpack('I',self.header_string[18:22])
    height = unpack('I',self.header_string[22:26])
    self.width = width[0]
    self.height = height[0]
    self.bit_map_dict = {}

    for self.y in range (0, self.height):
        for self.x in range (0,self.width):
            self.key= (self.x,self.y)
            self.pixel_list = []
            for c in range (0, 3):
                t=unpack('B', self.image_content_string[3 * (self.y * self.width + self.x) + c])
                self.pixel_list.append(t[0])
                self.bit_map_dict[self.key] = self.pixel_list

def write_file(self, out_file):
    out_string = self.header_string

    for y in range (0, self.height):
        for x in range (0, self.width):
            key=(x, y)
            for byte in range (0, 3):
                byte = pack('B', self.bit_map_dict[key][byte])
                out_string = out_string + byte

    output_file = open(out_file, 'w')
    output_file.write(out_string)
    output_file.close()
```

```python
if __name__ == '__main__':

    draw = BmpDraw('template_05_02.bmp')
    if draw.flag == 1:

        for x in range(0,draw.width):
            x_rad = radians(x*360.0/draw.width)
            y= int(0.5*draw.height + 0.5 * draw.height * sin(x_rad))
            draw.bit_map_dict[(x,y)] = [0,0,255]


        draw.write_file('output.bmp')
```

Prog 5 – 5

Prog 5 – 6 has also been saved on the CD as 'bmp_draw.py' the finished class. This can be imported and used to produce bit map images with content modified by software you write.


```python
#prog_05_06.py (bmpdraw.py)

from struct import *
from math import  *

class BmpDraw:

    def __init__(self, infile_name):
        self.infile_name = infile_name
        self.read_template()

    def read_template(self):
        try:
            template_file = open(self.infile_name, 'r')
            bit_map_string = template_file.read()
            template_file.close()
        except:
                self.flag = -1
                print 'Failed no template file!'
                return

        if bit_map_string[0:2] != 'BM':
            self.flag = -1
            print 'Failed not a .bmp!'
```

```
        return
    self.flag = 1
    self.header_string = bit_map_string[0:54]
    self.image_content_string = bit_map_string[54:]
    width=unpack('I', self.header_string[18:22])
    height=unpack('I', self.header_string[22:26])
    self.width = width[0]
    self.height = height[0]
    self.bit_map_dict = {}
    for self.y in range (0, self.height):
        for self.x in range (0, self.width):
            self.key=(self.x, self.y)
            self.pixel_list = []
            for c in range (0,3):
                t = unpack('B', self.image_content_string[3 * \
                (self.y * self.width+self.x) + c])
                self.pixel_list.append(t[0])
                self.bit_map_dict[self.key] = self.pixel_list

def line(self, x1, y1, x2, y2, colour):
    if x1 != x2:
        angle = atan2((y2-y1),(x2-x1))
    elif y2 > y1:
        angle = pi/2
    else:
        angle = 3 * pi/2
    length = int(sqrt((y2 - y1)**2+( x2 - x1) ** 2))
    for n in range (0,length):
        x=int(x1 + n * cos(angle))
        y=int(y1 + n * sin(angle))
        self.bit_map_dict[(x, y)] = colour

def poly(self, points, colour):
    l = len(points)
    for n in range (0, l ,2):
        x1=points[n]
        y1=points[n + 1]
        if n + 3 < l:
            x2 = points[n + 2]
            y2 = points[n + 3]
        else:
            x2=points[0]
            y2=points[1]
```

```python
            if x1 != x2:
                angle=atan2((y2-y1),(x2-x1))
            elif y2 > y1:
                angle=pi/2
            else:
                angle = 3 * pi/2
            length = int(sqrt((y2 - y1)**2+(x2 - x1) ** 2))
            for n in range (0, length):
                x=int(x1+n * cos(angle))
                y=int(y1 + n* sin(angle))
                self.bit_map_dict[(x, y)] = colour

    def arc(self, xc , yc, r , colour):
        step_angle = 1.0/r
        number_of_steps = int(r * 2 * pi)
        for n in range (0, number_of_steps):
            x = int(xc+r * cos(n * step_angle))
            y = int(yc+r * sin(n * step_angle))
            self.bit_map_dict[(x, y)]=colour
    def write_file(self,out_file):
            out_string = self.header_string
            for y in range (0, self.height):
                for x in range (0, self.width):
                    key = (x, y)
                    for byte in range (0, 3):
                        byte = pack('B',self.bit_map_dict[key][byte])
                        out_string = out_string + byte

            output_file=open(out_file, 'w')
            output_file.write(out_string)
            output_file.close()

if __name__ == '__main__':

    draw=BmpDraw('template_05_06.bmp')
    if draw.flag == 1:
        draw.arc(draw.width/2, draw.height/2, draw.height/4, [255, 0, 0])
        draw.line(0,0,draw.width,draw.height,[0, 0, 255])
        draw.poly([10,10,100,10,100,300],[100, 100, 100])
        draw.poly([20, 20, 200, 20, 200, 400, 20, 400], [255, 127, 0])

        draw.write_file('output.bmp')
```

Prog 5 – 6

It includes methods to draw lines given the x and y coordinates of the ends and the colour as a list. There is a method to draw polygons given the points and the colour, and a method to draw circles given the coordinates of the centre, the radius and the colour.

Chapter 6

More Hardware

6.1 Introduction

In chapter 3 the FTDI UM245R was introduced and a suggested circuit Fig 3 – 3 was given so that the programs would have something to work with. This chapter will contain more suggested circuits and a few programs to test them. So far we have only dealt with digital inputs, although they have been used to drive analogue meters where the input to the FTDI has been a single parallel byte. This chapter will deal with interfacing with a 12 bit analogue to digital converter the AD1286 and with driving outputs that, through a transistor, can switch external loads.

6.2 Circuit Board 2

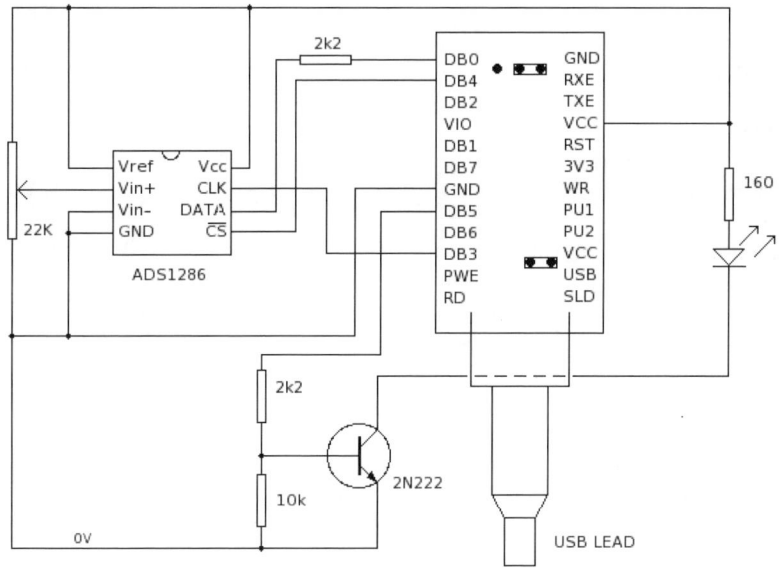

Fig 6 – 1

139

Fig 6 -1 shows a suggested circuit to experiment with digital outputs and analogue inputs. Only four of the input/outputs have been used; three are used to communicate with the ADS1286 A to D converter, a 12 bit serial device, the details will be dealt with later in the chapter. DB5 is used as a digital output to switch a transistor which here has an LED to drive from the USB 5V supply, but could switch up to 500mA from an external supply. The allocation of pins is as follows, DB0, DB1 and DB2 are inputs which will be for analogue data from A to D converters, DB3 and DB 4 are outputs to control the converters, and DB5, DB6 and DB7 are outputs to drive open collector transistors to switch external loads.

6.3 Digital outputs

The program Prog 6 – 1 is the heater controller from chapter 4, with a new class added called "DeviceB". Each instance of this class will be the interface to an FTDI for handling digital outputs and analog inputs. In chapter 3 the class "Device" was developed for digital inputs. This class will be included in a new file with other classes and called "ClassA".

```
#prog_06_01
from Tkinter import *
from _simple_ftdi import *

class FrontEnd():
    def __init__(self,master,devices):
        self.master=master
        self.devices=devices
        self.master.title('Heater Controller')
        self.but_on=Button(text='ON',command=self.on)
        self.but_off=Button(text='OFF',command=self.off)
        self.can_on_lamp=Canvas(width=40,height=40,bg='grey')
        self.can_off_lamp=Canvas(width=40,height=40,bg='red')
        self.lab_heater_switch=Label(text='HEATER\nSWITCH')
        self.lab_heater_on=Label(text='ON')
        self.lab_heater_off=Label(text='OFF')
        self.lab_heater_switch.grid(row=0,column=0,columnspan=2)
        self.lab_heater_off.grid(row=0,column=2,sticky='S')
        self.lab_heater_on.grid(row=0,column=3,sticky='S')

        self.but_off.grid(row=1,column=0,sticky='NW')
        self.but_on.grid(row=1,column=1,sticky='SE')
```

```
      self.can_off_lamp.grid(row=1,column=2,padx=10,pady=10)
      self.can_on_lamp.grid(row=1,column=3,padx=10,pady=10)

   def on(self):
      self.can_off_lamp.configure(bg='grey')
      self.can_on_lamp.configure(bg='green')
      self.devices[0].pins_on(32)
   def off(self):
      self.can_off_lamp.configure(bg='red')
      self.can_on_lamp.configure(bg='grey')
      self.devices[0].pins_off(32)

class DeviceB:
   handle=0
   def __init__(self,ftdi):
      self.ftdi=ftdi
      self.handle=DeviceB.handle
      DeviceB.handle=DeviceB.handle + 1
      self.device_up=open_device(self.ftdi,self.handle,248)

   def pins_on(self,mask):
      if self.device_up==0:
         self.state=read_pins(self.handle)
         self.state =self.state | mask
         self.state=write_pins(self.handle, self.state)

   def pins_off(self, mask):
      if self.device_up==0:
         self.state=read_pins(self.handle)
         self.state = self.state & ~mask
         write_pins(self.handle, self.state & ~mask)


interf1=DeviceB('FTCVMOYU')
root=Tk()
frontend=FrontEnd(root,[interf1])

root.mainloop()
```

Prog. 6 – 1

This new class will be developed further throughout the chapter. Only one instance of the class is created in this program "interf1". The __init__() method needs to have one argument passed to it, the serial number of the FTDI device as a string.

141

Again a class variable is used to generate an integer that will be the handle to the device. This class variable gets incremented every time an instance of "DeviceB" is created, but here there is only one. The "FrontEnd" class is the same as has been seen in chapter 4 except an extra argument is passed to the "__init__()" method which is a list of instances of class "DeviceB" that have been created. In class "DeviceB" the first three pins will be configured as inputs and the last five will be outputs. In the program the argument passed to the "open_device()" function to configure the pins is the integer 248.

The reason it is 248 is that in order to configure the pins as inputs or outputs (where an output is 1 and an input is 0) each pin's position has a binary weight, Table 6 – 1 shows this. Therefore if the last five pins are to be outputs the sum of the binary weights will be 248.

The reason it is 248 is that to configure the pins as inputs or outputs an output is 1 and an input is 0 each pin's position has a binary weight, Table 6 – 1 shows this. Therefore if the last five pins are to be outputs sum of the binary weights will be 248.

	DB0	DB1	DB2	DB3	DB4	DB5	DB6	DB7
Binary Weight	1	2	4	8	16	32	64	128

Table 6 – 1

Note that the "open_device()" function in "_simple_ftdi" initializes all outputs as off.

In the library simple_ftdi is a function "write_pins()". This function takes two arguments, the first is the handle to the device, the second is an integer calculated from the binary weights of those pins to be turned on. Suppose all the outputs are off and we want to turn on DB7, the code would be "write_pins(self.handle, 128)". But what if later on we want to turn on DB6 as well. Using "write_pins(self.handle,64)" would turn on DB6 but would also turn off DB7! What we have to do is read the state of the pins then modify the state with what we want to change and write this back to the device, READ MODIFY WRITE. There are two methods in the class "DeviceB" that do this called pins_on() and pins_off().

Here is the "pins_on()" method. First "self.state" is assigned to the integer that represents the state of the pins as they are. We want to turn on certain pins and leave the others unchanged. The variable "mask" is the integer that represents the pins that are to be turned on, and by using the bitwise Or (|) operator with these two variables "self.state" will be re-assigned to the required state of the pins for writing.

```
def pins_on(self,mask):
    if self.device_up==0:
        self.state=read_pins(self.handle)
        self.state =self.state | mask
        self.state=write_pins(self.handle, self.state)
```

Here as an example is the previously mentioned case involving DB6 and DB7

state before	10000000	128 decimal	the state with DB7 on
bitwise OR			
mask	01000000	64 decimal	mask to turn DB6 on
=	11000000	192 decimal	value written to the device

Turning pins off while leaving others unchanged is similar but requires an extra step.

```
def pins_off(self, mask):
    if self.device_up==0:
        self.state=read_pins(self.handle)
        self.state = self.state & ~mask
        write_pins(self.handle, self.state & ~mask)
```

Suppose we want to turn DB7 off and leave all the others unchanged. We use the bitwise "And" operator and a suitable mask. The state of the pins when they are read will be 11000000 and we want to turn the leftmost bit off and leave the others unchanged. Consider DB6, which is to be left on. If it's bit is "AND-ed" with a 1 this will give a 1. Now consider DB5 which is off and is to stay off. If it's bit which is 0 is "AND-ed" with a 1 this will give a 0. What about the bit we want to turn off = DB7? If it's bit is "AND-ed" with a 0 this will give 0.

Summarizing, bits that are to remain unchanged are "AND-ed" with a 1, bits that are to be turned off are "AND-ed" with a 0.

Now the argument "mask" passed to the method has the outputs we want off as 1s and the bits that we want unchanged as 0s, so all that is needed is to make all the 1s in the mask into 0s and all the 0s in the mask into 1s. An operator that does this is the bitwise invert "~".

mask   01000000   64 decimal mask to turn DB6 off, but needs to be inverted

~mask   10111111
bitwise AND
state before 11000000   192 decimal the state with DB7 and DB6 on

=   10000000   128 decimal value written to the device

In Prog. 6 – 1 the transistor is driven from pin DB5 which has a binary weight of 32; the code to turn it on and off are added to the "on()" and "off()" methods in "FrontEnd", they are "self.devices[0].pins_on(32)" and "self.devices[0].pins_off(32)". The "devices[0]" means the first device in the list of devices passed to "frontend.__init__()". Here there is only one device but there could be more.

6.4 Analog Input

By using an AD1286 that is a serial, analogue to digital converter it is possible to achieve 12 bit resolution using 3 input/outputs. Fig. 6 – 1 shows how the A/D converter is connected. It requires a 5V supply Vcc to ground that is obtained from the UM245R. A reference voltage for the converter is taken as Vcc. There are two analog input pins Vin+ and Vin-; Vin- is connected to ground and Vin+ is connected to the wiper of a potentiometer which spans Vcc to ground; it is the voltage on the potentiometer that will be converted.

Communication between the A to D converter and the FTDI device is achieved using a three wire bus.

On the UM245R one output pin is used as a clock which is connected to the clock input pin of the converter. The data output pin of the converter is connected to an input pin of the UM245 through a resistor in order to protect both devices in the event of the UM245's pin being accidentally configured as an output. Lastly, an output pin of the UM245 is connected to the chip select (CS) pin of the converter. Fig 6 – 2 shows how the data is clocked out of the converter.

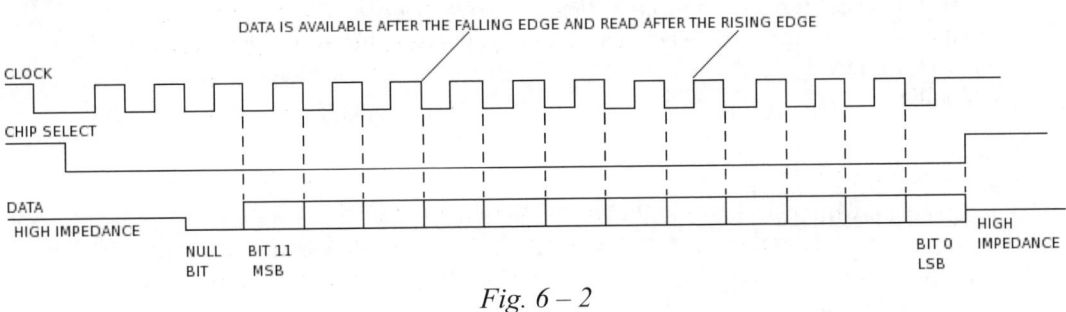

DATA IS AVAILABLE AFTER THE FALLING EDGE AND READ AFTER THE RISING EDGE

Fig. 6 – 2

Initially the clock and the chip select lines are high. The UM245R pulls the clock low and then the chip select low which initiates the conversion. The UM245R outputs two complete clock pulses, on the falling edge of the second clock pulse the data pin on the AD1286 changes from high impedance to outputting a null bit. At the next falling clock edge the most significant bit is available on the data pin, the bit is read by the UM245R on the next rising clock edge. This continues until all twelve bits have been clocked out and read. The clock then remains high and the chip select line is pulled high ready for the next conversion cycle, the data pin of the AD1286 reverts to high impedance.

Program 6 – 2 will display a slider that moves according to the position of the potentiometer in circuit Fig 6 – 1. The program creates an instance of a class FrontEnd which for this program has one slider that ranges from 0 to 4095 and its position is determined by the control variable "self.contvar1" which is an "IntVar()". The value of "self.contvar1" will be set by the output value of the analog to digital converter.

Class "DeviceB" is developed further here with the addition of the method "analog_in", this being the method that will clock out the data from the converter. Comments have been added to the program, these can be compared with Fig. 6 –2.

145

```
#prog_6_02.py

from Tkinter import *
from _simple_ftdi import *

class FrontEnd():
    def __init__(self, master, devices):
        self.master = master
        self.devices = devices  #List of devices
        self.master.title('Analog Input')
        self.contvar1 = IntVar()
        self.scale1 = Scale(orient = 'horizontal', length=800,\
        variable = self.contvar1, to = 4095, tickinterval = 500, bg = 'black' ,fg ='green')
        self.scale1.grid()
        self.poll()

    def poll(self):
        self.devices[0].analog_in()
        x1=self.devices[0].data0
        if x1 < 0:
            x1=0
            self.scale1.configure(fg = 'red',label = 'No Device')
        else:
            self.contvar1.set(x1)

        self.master.after(1,self.poll)

class  DeviceB:
    handle = 0
    def __init__(self,ftdi):
        self.ftdi = ftdi
        self.handle = DeviceB.handle
        DeviceB.handle = DeviceB.handle + 1
        self.device_up = open_device(self.ftdi,self.handle,248)
        self.clock = 8
        self.cs = 16
        if self.device_up == 0:
            self.pin_on(self.cs)
            self.pin_off(32)

    def pin_on(self, mask):
        if self.device_up == 0:
            self.state = read_pins(self.handle)
            self.state = write_pins(self.handle, self.state | mask)
```

146

```
def pin_off(self, mask):
    if self.device_up == 0:
        self.state = read_pins(self.handle)
        mask=mask ^ 0xff
        write_pins(self.handle, self.state & mask)

def analog_in(self):
    self.data0 = 0        #The three data inputs are data0, data1, and data2, here they are
                          #initialised to 0.
    self.data1 = 0
    self.data2 = 0
    if self.device_up == 0:
        self.pin_off(self.clock)              #Clock line pulled low.
        self.pin_off(self.cs)                 #chip select line pulled low.

        for n in range (0, 2):                #Two complete clock cycles.
            self.pin_on(self.clock)
            self.pin_off(self.clock)

        self.pin_on(self.clock)               #Rising edge part way through the null bit.


        for n in range (0, 12):               #12 data bits clocked out and read see main text
                          #for the full explanation.
            self.pin_off(self.clock)
            self.pin_on(self.clock)
            self.state = read_pins(self.handle)   #All pins are read after the rising
                          #clock edge.
            if self.state >= 0:
                self.data0 = self.data0 << 1      #All data bits are left shifted prior to
                          #the next significant bit being read.
            self.data1 = self.data1 << 1
            self.data2 = self.data2 << 1

            if self.state & 1: # Anding with data pin DB0
                          #Data input pin is checked to see
                          #if it is high
                self.data0 = self.data0 | 1           #If high data0 right most bit set.
            if self.state & 2: # Anding with data pin DB1
                self.data1 = self.data1 | 1
            if self.state & 4: # Anding with data pin DB2
                self.data2 = self.data2 | 1
```

```
        else:
            self.data0 = -1
            self.data1 = -1
            self.data2 = -1



    self.pin_on(self.cs)
        else:
            self.data0 = -1                          #The three data inputs are data0, data1, and data2,
                                                     #here they are initialised to 0.
            self.data1 = -1
            self.data2 = -1

interf1=DeviceB('FTCVMOYU')
root=Tk()
frontend = FrontEnd(root,[interf1])
root.mainloop()
```

Prog. 6 – 2

Clocking the data bits out is part of the job that "analog_in()" has, the other part is to assemble them as an integer. With the class "DeviceB" and it's associated circuit we have allowed for three analog inputs which means three ADS1286s. By using three separate data inputs pins on the UM245R we can simultaneously clock data from three ADS1286s by commoning the clock pins of the converters and also the CS pins. The converted values from the A to D converters will be "data0", "data1" and "data2", but as at the moment we have only one AD1286 in circuit the explanation will only mention "data0" from DB0.

Prior to clocking out the 12 data bits the variable "data0" is assigned to 0. When the "for n in range (0,12):" loop is entered, the clock line is high. The clock line is then set low which will make the most significant bit available on the data line. After the clock line is set high again the pins are read and "self.state" is assigned to their value. Now all the pins are read but we are only interested here in DB0 so if we bitwise "AND" "self.state" and the integer 1 the result will be true if DB0 is high. You will notice that all the bits in "data0" were shifted left 1 place prior to the bitwise "AND", this has no effect when data0 is 0. If DB0 is high we set the least significant bit of "data0" to 1. Subsequent times around the loop the left shift will move all the bits until the first bit read, which is the most significant bit, is at the left end of the 12 bit word. We now have "data0" assigned to the A to D value.

As an example suppose the converted analogue value is 2730 which in binary is 101010101010, this will be the bit pattern that will be clocked out of the data pin of the converter. The first bit clocked out will be the most significant bit therefore the state of the pins will be as follows.

DB0 = 1 (Bit 1, the most significant bit)
DB1 = 1 (Not connected, internal pull up in the FT245R makes it a 1)
DB2 = 1 (Not connected)
DB3 = 1 (Clock high during read)
DB4 = 0 (Chip select held low)
DB5 = 0 (Output off)
DB6 = 0 (Output off)
DB7 = 0 (Output off)

Therefore "self.state" will be 00001111, but we are only really interested in the value of DB0 here that is the rightmost bit. To test this bit we do a bitwise AND (&) with the integer 1.

00001111 & 00000001 = True

As this is true the right most bit of "data0" is set to 1 by the bitwise OR (|) with the integer 1. Initially "data0" is assigned to 0. Note that the integer 1 is shown here as only being eight bits but as all the bits are 0 except the least significant bit this does not matter.

data0   integer1
00000000 | 00000001 = 00000001

The next time round the loop the next significant bit is clocked out, bit 10.

Now "dat0" is left shifted by one bit.

00000001 << 1 = 00000010

The pins are read as this, which will be

DB0 = 0 (bit 10)
DB1 = 1 (Not connected, internal pull up in the FT245R makes it a 1)
DB2 = 1 (Not connected)
DB3 = 1 (Clock high during read)
DB4 = 0 (Chip select held low)
DB5 = 0 (Output off)

DB6 = 0 (Output off)
DB7 = 0 (Output off)

Again the DB0 is tested to see if it is high, as it is the bitwise OR gives this

00001110 & 00000001 = False

The next time round the loop the next significant bit is clocked out, bit 9.

Now "dat0" is left shifted by one bit.

00000010 << 1 = 00000100

This continues until all the bits have been read and "data0" will be 101010101010.

6.5 Alternative Functions

The library "_simple_ftdi" is very much a simplified set of functions and in particular when writing to the pins with "write_pins()" only one byte is sent. The library "libftdi" which is really doing the work has a function that can write multiple bytes which appear on the pins one after the other. "write_pins()" uses this function but only asks for one byte to be written, which is a very inefficient way to use USB. If you look at what has been happening, there is no need to read the pins during the first two clock cycles and the next rising edge; Therefore, these could be sent as a burst of bytes. Also. during the clocking out of the data bits the falling edge and the rising edge can be sent one after the other before a read is necessary. This has been implemented in the "_simple_ftdi" function "ads1286_read()" which takes one argument, the handle to the device and returns 0 if successful. The data for the input is accessed by another function "data_get()" which requires one argument, an integer 1, 2, or 3 which is the input you want the data for. The following lines of code will be added to the final development of class "DeviceB"


```
def ads1286(self):          #Optional faster method uses C functions in _simple_ftdi
    if self.device_up==0:
        ads1286_read(self.handle)
        self.data0=data_get(0)
        self.data1=data_get(1)
        self.data2=data_get(2)
    else:
```

```
self.data0=-1
self.data1=-1
self.data2=-1
```

The line "self.devices[0].analog_in()" in method "poll()" would be replaced by "self.devices[0].ads1286()".

6.6 Reference Voltage

The A to D converter output is a number between 0 and 4095 where this range represents 0 volts to Vref. In Fig. 6 – 1 we used Vcc, the 5V supply, as V ref. Now, while this works where the Vin is derived from a potentiometer connected across Vcc, as Vcc varies we still get the same proportional reading. If we want to use the converter as a voltmeter the Vref must be constant. Fig. 6 – 3 is a circuit to drive a regulated reference voltage. An LM723 voltage regulator has a reference output of approximately 7.15 V, this means that the voltage will vary from chip to chip but will be constant for individual chips; the range quoted on the data sheet is 6.95V to 7.35V. The chip has also an operational amplifier capable of supplying 25 mA, but as the reference output can supply 15mA we will use this directly. The supply voltage to the LM723 must be at least 9.5V, this is provided by the ADM660 voltage doubler - the lowest voltage from the USB should not be lower than 4.75 which would still be within limits for the worst case.

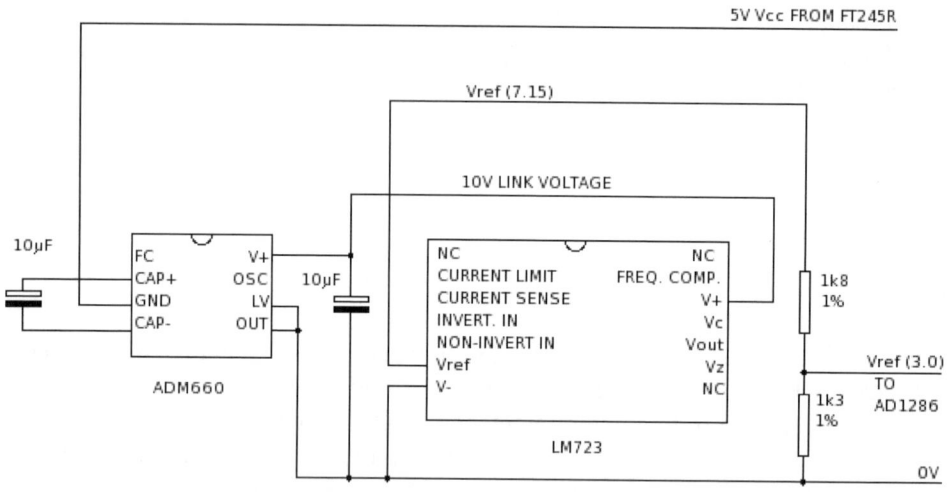

Fig. 6 − 3

The connections shown on the ADM660 show how it is connected as a doubler. It can also be used to produce a negative output equal to the input voltage. Note, as a doubler the GND is connected to Vcc. After allowing for the tolerance of Vref and the 1% resistors the reference voltage to the A to D converters will be between 2.86 and 3.14 volts, these are the extremes if all three tolerances produced a worst result. The voltage applied to the Vref pin of the ADS1286 should not be greater than Vcc+0.05V and the input voltage to Vin+ should not exceed Vref by more than 0.2V.

6.7 Temperature Sensor

To measure temperatures between -10 and 125 degrees C the MCP9701 active thermistor can easily be used.

This sensor is a three wire device, 5V supply, ground and an output that is 400mV at 0 degrees C rising by 19.5mV per degree C. The sensors are very inexpensive and currently cost about £5 for a bag of 20 in the UK. Temperature sensing will be the subject of the next chapter.

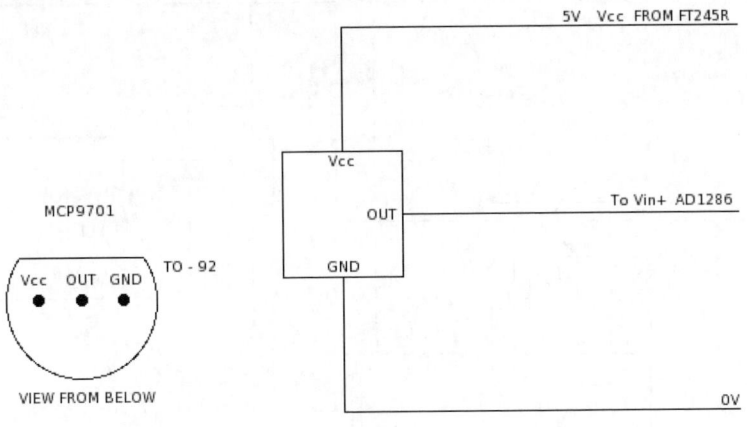

Fig. 6 – 4

6.8 Switching Larger Currents

While discussing digital outputs only an LED supplied by the USB was switched on and off. Larger loads need to be supplied by an external power supply. Fig. 6 – 5 shows a method of interfacing a larger load to the USB interface board. Electrically the interface board is isolated from the power board by the opto-isolator SFH-6182. The phototransistor in the isolator conducts because of infrared from the integrated LED. When the driving output is high, approximately 1.6mA will flow in the LED; the current transfer ratio at this level of forward current is over 100%. This will give sufficient drive to turn on the 2N222 and energize RL1. The main load that we want to control is switched by the relay contacts.

When the transistor switches off the collapsing magnetic field in the relay coil induces an electro motive force (EMF) that tries to maintain the current flow, this is Lenz's Law. By having a reverse biased diode connected across the coil this current can flow through the diode dissipating the energy that was in the magnetic field as heat in the circuit comprising the relay and the diode. Without this diode the collapsing field would induce a high voltage spike that could damage the transistor and other semiconductor devices in circuit.

WARNING:
Do not use this circuit to switch higher voltages unless you have the necessary experience and can comply with the wiring regulations in your country.

153

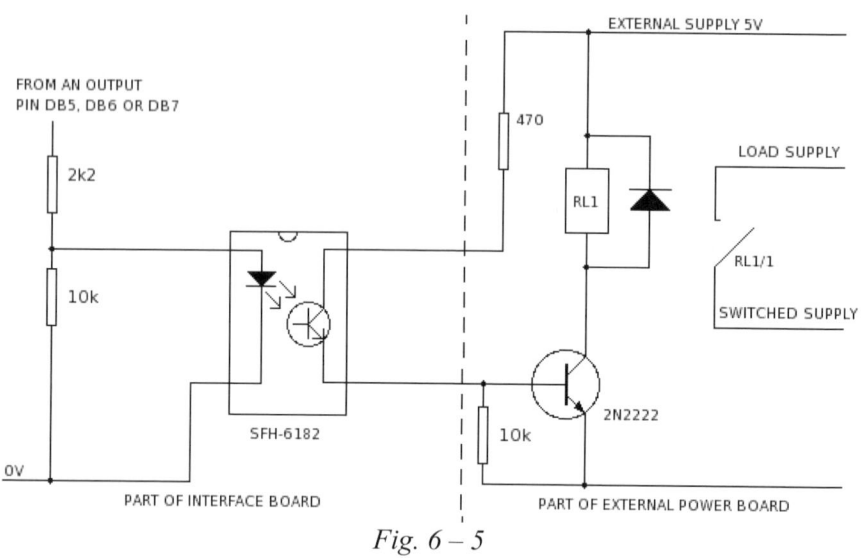

Fig. 6 – 5

6.9 Watchdog Circuit

There is a major flaw in the arrangement shown by Fig 6 – 5. If the program stops running with the output high then RL1 will remain energized. Something needs to be put in place to de-energize all outputs when the program stops. In industrial control systems that use programmable logic controllers (PLCs) one method of monitoring a program to ensure that it is still running is to have a digital output producing pulses which are monitored by a hardware timer device. The timer device sends out an alarm signal if the output stops changing state. We don't need to set aside a separate output as we already have CS and CLOCK that can give regular pulses. Fig 6 – 6 shows the so-called 'watchdog circuit'. Instead of taking the cathode connections of the opto-isolators directly to 0V they will be taken to 0V through transistor TR1. IC1 is a retriggerable monostable; a rising edge from CS causes an approximate two and half second pulse from the output on pin 13 that turns on TR1. Further rising edges within the time of the output pulse extends the pulse. Providing CS does not stop producing pulses the output remains high and the opto-isolators remain enabled. If the program ends then pin 13 will go low two and a half seconds after the last rising edge from CS, turning off TR1 and disabling the opto isolators. It is necessary to ground all the pins as shown, this device has two monostables and the other will generate noise if pin 11 is not grounded. Diode D1 is there to protect the monostable from the discharge current from C1 when the power supply is turned off.

154

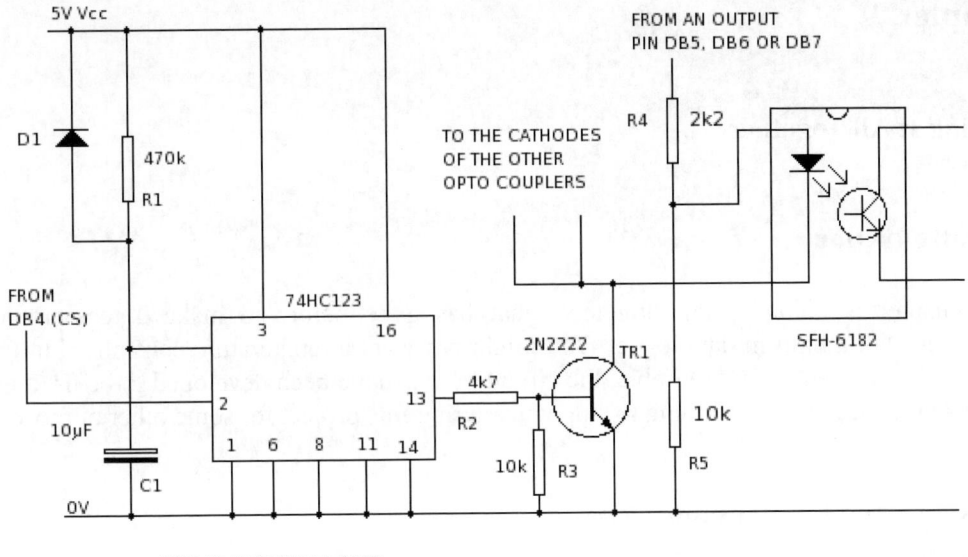

PART OF INTERFACE BOARD

Fig. 6 – 6

Chapter 7

Putting It All Together

7.1 Introduction

This chapter is going to pull together what has gone before to make a temperature controller with a built in data logger. You might not want a temperature controller but the code is object oriented and reusable, the circuit boards have been developed to be used for various purposes, there is nothing to stop you altering this project for some other purpose..

7.2 Hide Away the Reusable Code

New projects you write don't have to have long lengths of code on display. If all the source codes for the classes that have been written are put in one file we can just import this one file and use the methods.

Back in chapter 4 when class "Meter0" was developed we were using switches to present a parallel byte to the UM245R. Now that class "DevicesB" is available with analog inputs class Meter0 will be altered to simplify its use. Firstly it is now called "Meter" to prevent confusion. Some of the arguments passed to it have changed, they are now, "zero_offset" which allows the dial to start at a value other than zero, "fsd" has been replaced by "span" which is the full deflection range of the needle, the others remain the same except the serial number of a device is no longer required. The method "read_device()" is now called "deflect()" which is passed one argument "signal" that is an integer between 0 and 4095 to match the resolution of the analog inputs. There are also some minor alterations to the calculations to distribute the graduations and scale numbers because of the zero offset. Program listing Prog 7 – 1 shows the revised class.

```
#prog_07_01.py

class Meter(Canvas):
    def __init__(self, side, zero_offset, span, grad_maj, grad_min, units):
        self.zero_offset = zero_offset
        self.side = side
        self.span = span
```

```python
        self.grad_maj = grad_maj
        self.grad_min = grad_min
        self.units = units
        self.reading = 0
        self.orig = self.side/2.0
        self.R = 0.95*self.side/2
        self.r = 0.9*self.side/2
        self.num_r = 0.8*self.side/2
        self.can_meter = Canvas(height = self.side,width = self.side,bg = '#707070')
        self.can_meter.create_oval(self.orig - self.R, self.orig - self.R,\
        self.orig + self.R, self.orig + self.R,width=3,fill='#ffffff')
        for n in range (0, self.span+1):
            alpha_deg = (225 - n*270/self.span)
            alpha = radians(alpha_deg)
            if n%self.grad_min == 0:
                y = self.R*sin(alpha)
                x = self.R*cos(alpha)
                self.can_meter.create_line(self.orig,self.orig,self.orig+x,self.orig - y)
            if n%self.grad_maj == 0:
                y = self.R*sin(alpha)
                x = self.R*cos(alpha)
                self.can_meter.create_line(self.orig, self.orig, self.orig + x, self.orig \
                - y, fill = '#ff0000', width = 3)

        self.can_meter.create_oval(self.orig-self.r, self.orig-self.r, self.orig+self.r,\
        self.orig+self.r, fill='#ffffff')

        for n in range (self.zero_offset, self.span + self.zero_offset + 1):
            alpha_deg=(225 - (n - self.zero_offset) * 270.0/self.span)
            alpha=radians(alpha_deg)
            if n%self.grad_maj == 0:
                y = self.num_r * sin(alpha)
                x = self.num_r * cos(alpha)
                self.can_meter.create_text(self.orig + x,self.orig - y, text = str(n))

        self.can_meter.create_text(self.orig, self.orig * 1.5, text = self.units)

def deflect(self,signal):
        try:
            self.can_meter.delete(self.spindle)
            self.can_meter.delete(self.needle)
        except:
            pass
```

157

```
self.reading_r = signal
if self.reading_r < 0:
   self.reading_r = -500

self.reading = self.reading+(self.reading_r - self.reading)/5.0          #Needle damping
alpha_deg=(225 - self.reading*270.0/4095)
alpha=radians(alpha_deg)
beta=radians(135)
ax = self.orig + 0.025 * self.side * cos(alpha-beta)
ay = self.orig - 0.025 * self.side*sin(alpha-beta)
bx = self.orig + 0.025*self.side*cos(alpha+beta)
by = self.orig-0.025*self.side*sin(alpha+beta)
cx = self.orig+self.r*cos(alpha)
cy = self.orig-self.r*sin(alpha)
self.needle = self.can_meter.create_polygon(ax,ay,bx,by,cx,cy)
self.spindle = self.can_meter.create_oval(self.orig-.01*self.side,\
self.orig -0.01 * self.side, self.orig + 0.01 * self.side, self.orig + \
0.01 * self.side, fill = '#ffffff')
```

Prog 7 - 1

This class along with 'DevicesA' and 'DevicesB' is in 'interface_classes.py' on the downloadable CD.

7.3 Temperature Gauge

Fig. 7 – 1 shows a circuit for a single channel temperature instrument using an MCP9701 as the sensor. The sensor can be soldered to a length of screened cable and the soldered joints and the legs of the sensor potted in something like Araldite glue to allow it to be used remotely and for its immersion in water if desired. Prog 7 – 1 is the listing for this instrument. A calibration can be achieved by measuring your reference voltage and inserting it in the program, in the line that scales the raw output from the converter to voltage, mine was 3019 mV

To calculate the temperature the raw output is converted to mV and the variable "voltage" is assigned to this value. Then 400 mV, which is the sensors output at 0 degrees C is subtracted, the result is divided by 19.5 which gives the temperature above 0.

```
#prog_07_02.py

from interface_classes import *

class FrontEnd():
    def __init__(self,master,devices):
        self.master = master
        master.title('Temperature Controller')
        self.devices = devices
        self.meter1 = Meter(500, -10, 60, 10, 2, "Degrees C")
        self.meter1.can_meter.grid(row = 0, column = 0, rowspan = 2)
        self.read_temp()

    def read_temp(self):
        self.devices[0].ads1286()
        raw=self.devices[0].data0
        if raw < 0:
            signal = -1
        else:
            voltage = 3019.0 * raw/4095
            temperature = (voltage -400)/19.5
            signal = (temperature + 10) * 4095/60

        self.meter1.deflect(signal)
        self.master.after(1, self.read_temp)

root = Tk()
interf1 = DeviceB('FTCVMOYU')
frontend = FrontEnd(root, [interf1])
root.mainloop()
```

Prog 7 - 2

159

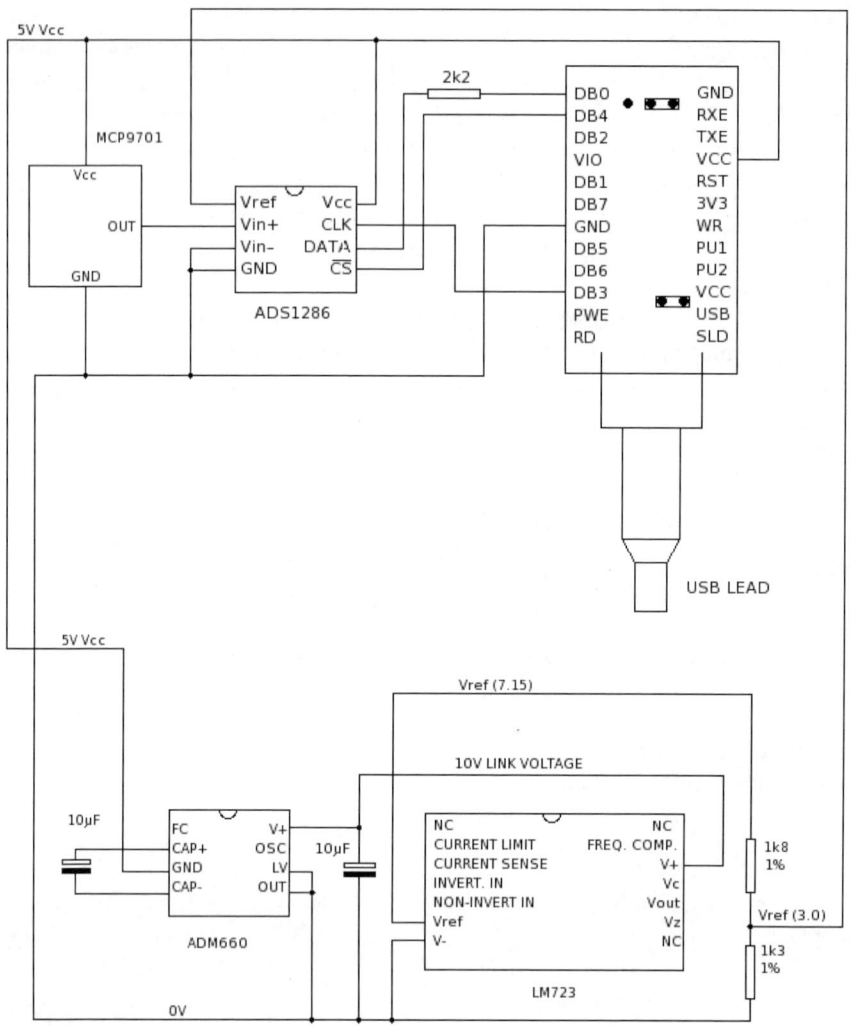

Fig. 7 - 1

7.4 A Better Calibration

Calibrating by simply entering the measured reference voltage is not a good calibration as this does not take into account errors in the sensor. It is better to measure at least two known temperatures and record the raw converter outputs and then it is just arithmetic to get degrees C. If we consider the sensor's response to be linear, it would appear from the data sheet that it is to within a degree between 0 and 100 degrees C and we can use the equation for a straight line. See Fig 7 – 2 that shows a typical relationship between temperature and raw output, m is the slope of the line and c is the vertical offset of the line or the point where it crosses the vertical axis, note c has a negative value here.

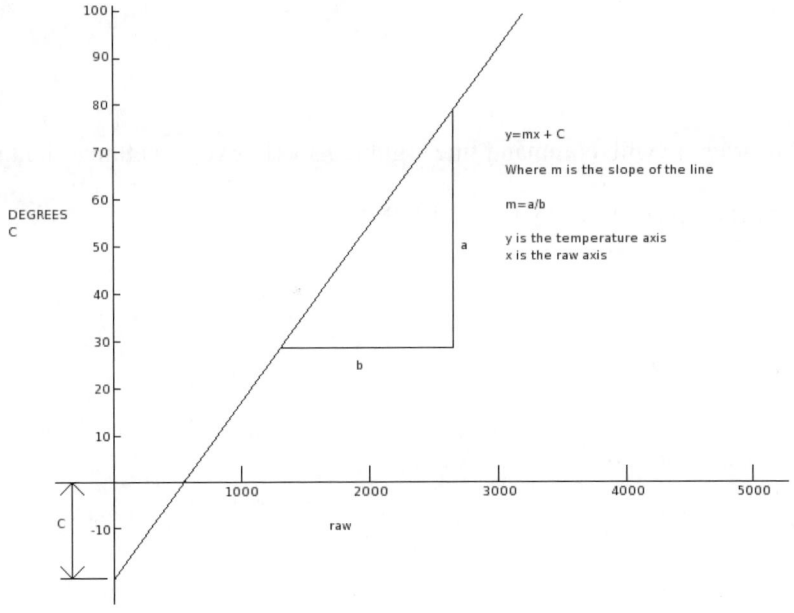

Fig. 7 – 2

We could incorporate a calibration routine into the instrument software but this would complicate the program for something that is only to be done occasionally. Instead Prog 7 – 4 is a program just for calibrating temperature sensor inputs - it will give values for "m" and "c" which can be manually entered into the code. Also the code for calculating the temperature will have to be modified as we will no longer need to know anything about

Vref. The calibrator program will not be a Tkinter GUI but instead a command line program. It is worth remembering that a command line program is quicker to write for tools like this. With command line programs you can pass variables from the command line. Prog 7 – 3 is a very short program to play with to demonstrate how this works. The "sys" module has to be imported, "argv" is a list of all the command line arguments which are typed after the program name. All the program here does is to print "argv". Each command line argument is typed without quotation marks and separated by at least one space. Each argument becomes a string in the list "argv". The first member of the list "argv[0]" is the name of the program.

```
#prog_07_03.py

from sys import *

print argv
```

Prog 7 - 3

Running this program with command line arguments will give something like this.

```
root@slax:~# python prog_07_03.py 1 two III 100
['prog_07_03.py', '1', 'two', 'III', '100']
root@slax:~#
```

```
#prog_07_04.py (calibrator.py)

#command line args -- prog_07_04.py, serial number, input number, low temp, high temp
from interface_classes import *
from sys import *
from time import *

def read():
    raw_average = 0
    raw_average_last = 2
    while (raw_average - raw_average_last) ** 2 > 1:
        raw_average_last = raw_average
        raw_total = 0
        for n in range (0, 100):
            board.ads1286()
            if argv[2] == '0':
                raw = board.data0
            elif argv[2] == '1':
```

162

```python
            raw=board.data1
        elif argv[2] == '2':
            raw = board.data2
        else:
            print argv[2] + ' Command line argument, incorrect pin number'
            sys.exit()
        raw_total = raw_total + raw

        raw_average = raw_total/100.0
        print raw_average

    raw_average = (raw_average + raw_average_last)/2
    return raw_average

if len(argv) != 5:
    print '\n\nIncorrect command line arguments - Must be the serial number' \
    ' of one UM245R and the input (0, 1, or 2) and high temp and low temp.\n\n'
    sys.exit()

lo_temp = 1.0*int(argv[3])
hi_temp = 1.0*int(argv[4])
board = DeviceB(argv[1])
if board.device_up != 0:
    print '\n\nFailed to open FTDI device serial number ' + argv[1] + '\n\n'
    sys.exit()

print 'Apply low reference temperature and press return.'
raw_input()
low_raw = read()
print 'Apply high reference temperature and press return.'
raw_input()
high_raw = read()

try:
    m=(hi_temp - lo_temp)/(high_raw-low_raw)
    c=lo_temp - m*low_raw
except:
    print '\n\nCalibration Failed.\n\n'
    sys.exit()
output_string = 'Serial = %s m = %f      c = %f' % (argv[1], m, c)
file_name=argv[1] + '_cal.dat'
file=open(file_name,'w')
file.write(output_string)
file.close()
```

print output_string

Prog 7 – 4

Prog 7 – 4 requires four command line arguments; the serial number of the UM245R, the input number of the analog input, the low reference temperature and the high reference temperature. The program has one function that will be called to return the raw output of the converter at required temperatures. When the program runs, a check is carried out to ensure that "argv" has five members, the name of the program and the four added arguments. If this is false the program prints an error message and ends. An instance of the class "DeviceB" is created called "board" with the serial number argument provided by "argv[1]" which is our first given command line argument. A message telling the user to apply the low reference temperature is given and the program then pauses with the built in function "raw_input" With the sensor at the low temperature the program continues after the user presses return. The variable "low_raw" is assigned to the returned float from the function "read()". This function has a loop taking an average of 100 readings. At the start of each loop the value of the last average is assigned to "average_last" and a new average of 100 hundred readings is taken. The outer "while" loop continues until two successive averages are within 1 of each other. This is determined by squaring the difference to always make it positive. The final returned float is the average of these two averages. This is repeated for the variable "high_raw" which is achieved at the higher temperature. The equations for calculating the slope and the offset are derived in Fig 7 - 3.

```
Let y1 be the low reference temperature
Let y2 be the high reference temperature
Let x1 be the raw output at the low reference temperature
Let x2 be the raw output at the high reference temperature
Let m be the slope
Let c be the offset

y1 = mx1 + c   (Equation 1)
y2 = mx2 + c   (Equation 2)

y2 - y1 = mx2 + c - mx1 - c  (Equation 2 - Equation 1)

y2 - y1 = m(x2 - x1)


m = (y2 - y1)/(x2 - x1)


Now that m is known, using either Equation 1 or 2


c = y1 - mx1          or          c = y2 - mx2
```

Fig. 7 – 3

Now to apply this to Prog. 7 – 2 replace the lines shown by the following code snippet.

```
voltage = 3019.0 * raw/4095              #Remove
temperature = (voltage -400)/19.5        #Remove
signal = (temperature + 10) * 4095/60    #Remove

temperature=self.m*raw+self.c            #Insert
signal=(temperature+10)*4095/60          #Insert
```

Prog 7 – 5   (Part of)

Prog 7 – 5 is the same as Prog 7 - 2 except for these lines, it is on CD.

Fig 7 – 4 below shows the completed single channel controller, with data logged every 30 seconds, the program is Prog 7 – 6, and the schematic diagram is Fig 7 – 5.

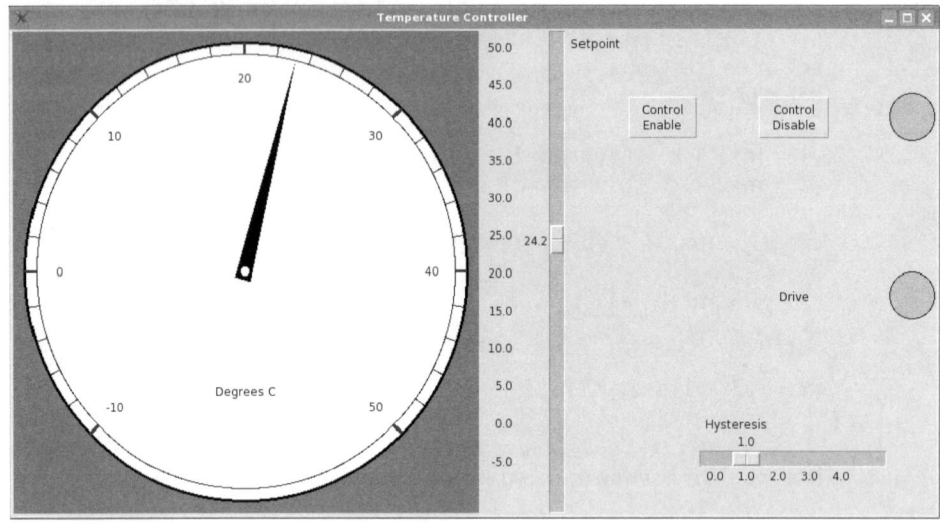

Fig. 7 – 4

#prog_07_06.py

from interface_classes import *
from pickle import *
from time import *

```python
class FrontEnd():
    def __init__(self, master, devices):
        self.master = master
        master.title('Temperature Controller')
        self.devices = devices
        self.enable_flag = False
        self.log_flag = False
        self.var_setpoint = DoubleVar()
        self.var_hyst = DoubleVar()
        self.var_log = IntVar()
        self.meter1 = Meter(500,-10,60,10,2,"Degrees C")
        self.scale1 = Scale(orient = 'vertical', length = 500,label = "Setpoint",from_ = 50,\
        to = -10, tickinterval = 5, resolution = 0.1, variable = self.var_setpoint, command =
```

166

```
        self.save_settings)
            self.button_enable = Button(text = 'Control\nEnable', command = self.enable)
            self.button_disable = Button(text = 'Control\nDisable', command = self.disable)
            self.can_enable = Canvas(width = 50, height = 50)
            self.lab_drive = Label(text = 'Drive')
            self.can_drive = Canvas(width = 50, height = 50)
            self.enable_ind = self.can_enable.create_oval(1, 1, 49, 49, fill = '#ff0000')
            self.drive_ind=self.can_drive.create_oval(1, 1, 49, 49, fill= '#ff0000')
            self.scale_hyst=Scale(orient = 'horizontal', length = 200, from_ = 0, to = 5, tickinterval = 1,\
            resolution = 0.1, variable = self.var_hyst,label = 'Hysteresis', command = self.save_settings)

            self.meter1.can_meter.grid(row = 0,column = 0,rowspan = 3)
            self.scale1.grid(row = 0, column = 1, rowspan = 3)
            self.button_enable.grid(row = 0, column = 2)
            self.button_disable.grid(row = 0, column = 3)
            self.can_enable.grid(row = 0, column = 4)
            self.lab_drive.grid(row = 1, column = 3)
            self.can_drive.grid(row = 1, column = 4)
            self.scale_hyst.grid(row = 2, column = 3, rowspan = 2)
            self.temperature_average = 0

            self.m = 0.033364
            self.c = -27.877019
            try:
                file_name = self.devices[0].ftdi + '_settings.dat'
                file = open(file_name, 'r')
                settings = load(file)
                file.close()
                self.var_setpoint.set(settings[0])
                self.var_hyst.set(settings[1])
            except:
                pass
            self.start = time()

            self.read_temp()

    def read_temp(self):
        self.devices[0].ads1286()
        raw=self.devices[0].data0
        if raw < 0:
            signal = -1
        else:
            self.temperature = self.m * raw+self.c
            self.temperature_average = (self.temperature_average * 49+self.temperature)/50.0
```

167

```python
        signal = (self.temperature_average + 10) * 4095/60

        self.meter1.deflect(signal)
        setpoint = self.var_setpoint.get()
        hyst = self.var_hyst.get()

        if self.enable_flag and setpoint - hyst/1.0 > self.temperature_average:
            self.devices[0].pin_on(32)
            self.can_drive.delete(self.drive_ind)
            self.drive_ind = self.can_drive.create_oval(1,1,49,49,fill='#00ff00')
        if self.enable_flag == False or self.temperature_average > setpoint:
            self.devices[0].pin_off(32)
            self.can_drive.delete(self.drive_ind)
            self.drive_ind = self.can_drive.create_oval(1,1,49,49,fill= '#ff0000')
        self.log()
        self.master.after(1,self.read_temp)


    def enable(self):
        self.enable_flag = True
        self.can_enable.delete(self.enable_ind)
        self.enable_ind = self.can_enable.create_oval(1,1,49,49,fill='#00ff00')

    def disable(self):
        self.enable_flag = False
        self.can_enable.delete(self.enable_ind)
        self.enable_ind = self.can_enable.create_oval(1,1,49,49,fill = '#ff0000')

    def save_settings(self,val):
        file_name = self.devices[0].ftdi + '_settings.dat'
        setpoint = self.var_setpoint.get()
        hyst = self.var_hyst.get()
        file = open(file_name, 'w')
        dump([setpoint,hyst], file)
        file.close()


    def log(self):
        if time() - self.start > 30:
            self.start = time()
            file_name = self.devices[0].ftdi + '_log.csv'
            file = open(file_name, 'a')
            file.write(ctime() + ',' + '%0.2f' % (self.temperature_average) + '\n')
```

168

```
            file.close()


root = Tk()
interf1 = DeviceB('FTCVMOYU')
frontend = FrontEnd(root, [interf1])
root.mainloop()
```

Prog 7 – 6

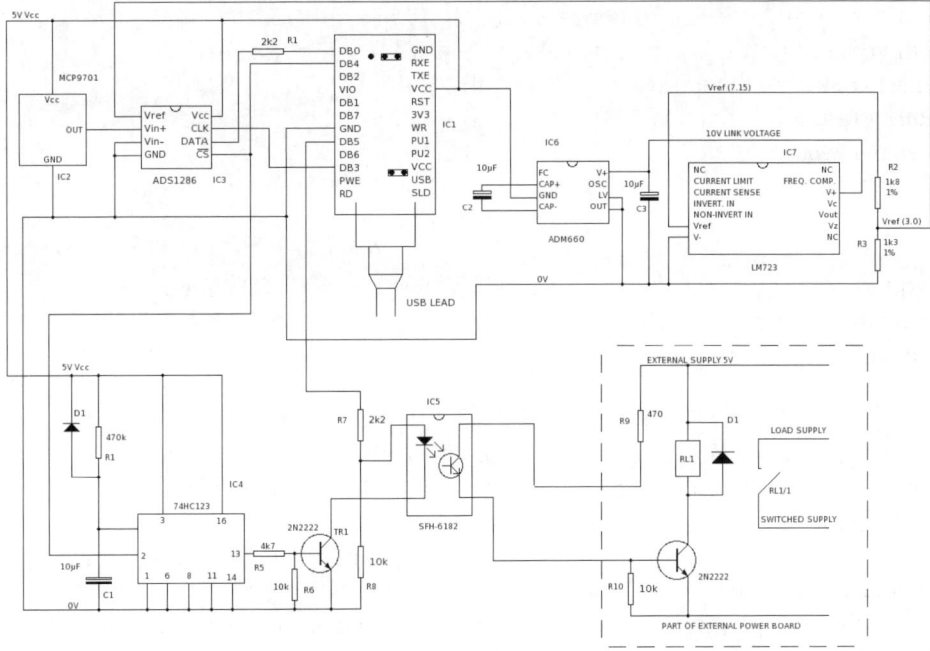

Fig. 7 – 5

This project combines many topics from throughout the book. The data logging has been simplified to one function of a few lines that writes to a file with the device serial number in the name. Any adjustment to the setpoint or hysteresis is immediately pickled to a file and the settings are reloaded next time the program runs. The circuit above has already been produced in parts. The external power board should be electrically isolated from the computer interface with its own power supply. This is for reasons of safety, noise and the limit on USB current draw. The external supply does not have to be 5V as long as the relay is appropriately rated and the collector emitter voltages of the transistors are not exceeded. Fig 7 –6 shows the circuit development board for "DevicesB".

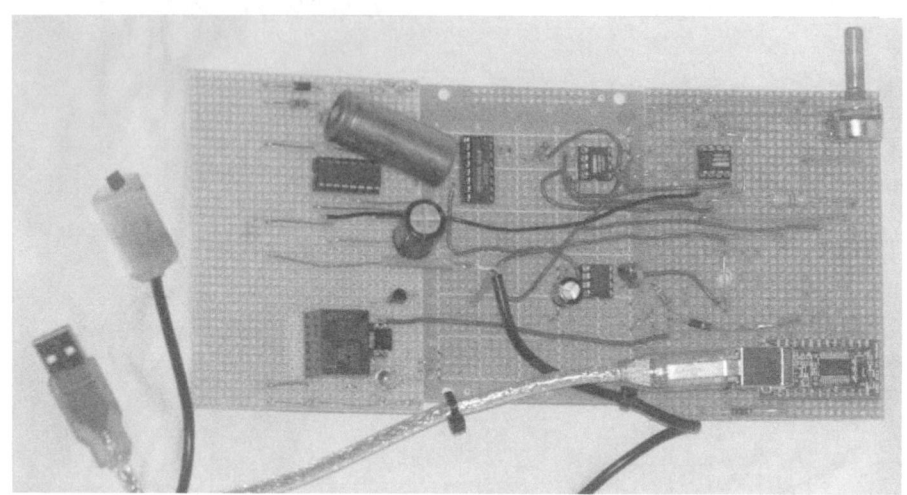

Fig. 7 – 6

Chapter 8

Getting the Apache Web Server Up

8.1 Introduction

So far we have dealt with interfacing with hardware that is local to the computer we are using. By setting up a local area network you can interface with equipment from a different computer. By using the Internet this can be the other side of the world. This chapter will deal with networking between a server and clients. This will allow the hardware plugged into the computer that is running the server to be controlled and monitored from any other computer using a standard web browser. When we use the FTDI chips we don't have to know the details of USB at a low level, this is thanks to the "libftdi" by Thomas Jarosch of Intra2net. With networking between computers we can use "TCP IP" again without worrying about the low level details. The apache web server will take care of the details of the data transmission, what needs to be done is the configuring of the server, setting up IP addresses, and the writing of Python code that will run on the server to interface with our hardware. In chapter 9 we will deal with hyper text makeup language (html), to create web pages, again the treatment of this will very basic, chapter 10 will be using Python running on the server to generate html scripts.

8.2 Networking

The CD already has the apache web server installed, slax has been configured to start the server at boot time so to check to see if it is working open the web browser Firefox or "konquerer" and type in the address bar either "http://localhost" or "http://127.0.0.1". You will see the message "It works!". The apache web server has a default web page in the folder "/usr/local/apache2/htdocs/" that generates this, the file is "index.html" The contents of this file are shown below in Prog 8 – 1. If you navigate to this file with "kate" you can change the test to something else. It is a good idea to change this message now so that later on it will prove it is coming from the server on this computer.

```
<html><body><h1>It works!</h1></body></html>
```

Prog 8 – 1 (/usr/local/apache2/htdocs/index.html)

In order to access the server from another computer we need to set up a network, two methods will be described the first is the "ad-hoc" wireless network which allows computers to communicate with each other as peer to peer. You need two computers with Wi-Fi cards. The examples given here are for a desktop computer with a D-Link USB Wi-Fi dongle, and a Dell laptop. Fig 8 – 1 shows the physical setup. The figure shows the desktop computer that has the FT245R plugged in also being connected through an ethernet lead to a wireless router that is serving other computers in the house. The network of interest is the ad-hoc network to the lap top. This ad-hoc network is separate from the LAN.

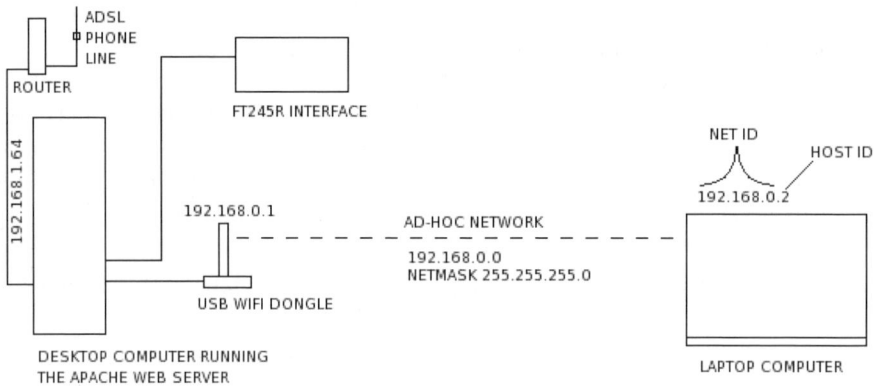

Fig 8 – 1

8.3 IP Addressing

The IP address is a 32 bit number, to make this more human friendly the 32 bits are expressed by four decimal numbers from 0 to 255 separated by a dot, each decimal number is eight of the bits. Fig 8 – 1 shows a desktop computer with a USB wifi interface networked with a laptop that has its own Wi-Fi interface. The two interfaces each have a different IP address. In this case "192.168.0.1" and "192.168.0.2". There are two parts to the IP address, the net id, and the host id. The host id is the address of that host on the net, in our case the last eight bits. The net id is the rest of the IP address. This is a class C IP address where the net is identified by a 24 bit number which must start with "110" as the first 3 bits "11000000" is 192. The host cannot use 0 or 255 as its address. The diagram shows the netmask which here is "255.255.255.0" this number specifies which bits make up the network id, all the bits that are 1 are the bits in the IP address that make up the network id. This is as far as we need to go with this.

8.4 The Ad-Hoc Network

Setting up an ad-hoc network is very easy in Linux and can be done from the command line. There are only three commands to use but they take a few options to set things up. The commands are "ifconfig" , "iwconfig" and "iwlist". Below is how to set up the ad-hoc network between two computers.

Firstly on the desktop computer with the D-Link USB interface "iwlist scanning" will tell you what is the name of your interface and if any other networks are within range.

root@slax:~# iwlist scanning
lo   Interface doesn't support scanning.

eth0   Interface doesn't support scanning.

wmaster0 Interface doesn't support scanning.

wlan0   Scan completed :
          Cell 01 - Address: 00:18:F6:AC:3F:41
                  ESSID:"BTHomeHub-C76A"
                  Mode:Master
                  Channel:7
                  Frequency:2.442 GHz (Channel 7)
                  Quality=54/100 Signal level:-34 dBm
                  Encryption key:on
                  Bit Rates:1 Mb/s; 2 Mb/s; 5.5 Mb/s; 11 Mb/s; 18 Mb/s
                      24 Mb/s; 36 Mb/s; 54 Mb/s; 6 Mb/s; 9 Mb/s
                      12 Mb/s; 48 Mb/s
                  Extra:tsf=0000004be3c88008
                  Extra: Last beacon: 376ms ago

root@slax:~#

The results tell us that the interface is "wlan0" and there is a network within range, which we are not actually interested in. If you get a result like this below, it means that "wlan0" is there but down, we have still got the information we want. It won't always be "wlan0".

173

```
root@slax:~# iwlist scanning
lo        Interface doesn't support scanning.

eth0      Interface doesn't support scanning.

wmaster0  Interface doesn't support scanning.

wlan0     Interface doesn't support scanning : Network is down
```

Now we need to configure "wlan0" as our ad-hoc network, we need to give it a network name known as "essid",
Extended Service Set ID, and if you want to you can encrypt the network. The command to configure the wireless interface is "iwconfig" but before that the interface has to be down, for which we use "ifconfig" as follows.

```
root@slax:~# ifconfig wlan0 down
root@slax:~#
```

Now to configure it.

```
root@slax:~# iwconfig wlan0 essid the_network mode ad-hoc key 6789abcdef
root@slax:~#
```

I have called the network "the_network" the mode is ad-hoc and the key is "6789abcdef" (the key can be any ten hexadecimal digits). Then by using "iwconfig" on its own you can check that everything is set as you want it. If anything has not been set run the above instruction again, remember at the command line you can easily recall instructions using the up arrow key, and go forward through instructions using the down arrow key.

```
root@slax:~# iwconfig
lo        no wireless extensions.

eth0      no wireless extensions.

wmaster0  no wireless extensions.

wlan0     IEEE 802.11bg  ESSID:"the_network"
```

Mode:Ad-Hoc Frequency:2.412 GHz Cell: Not-Associated
Tx-Power=13 dBm
Retry min limit:7 RTS thr:off Fragment thr=2352 B
Encryption key:6789-ABCD-EF
Power Management:off
Link Quality:0 Signal level:0 Noise level:0
Rx invalid nwid:0 Rx invalid crypt:0 Rx invalid frag:0
Tx excessive retries:0 Invalid misc:0 Missed beacon:0

root@slax:~#

Now that interface is set up we use "ifconfig" to set an IP address for this host. To do this "ifconfig -a" will list all the interfaces both wireless and wired so we can choose a network id that is different.

root@slax:~# ifconfig -a
eth0   Link encap:Ethernet HWaddr 00:15:58:62:59:89
          inet addr:192.168.1.64 Bcast:192.168.1.255 Mask:255.255.255.0
          BROADCAST NOTRAILERS MULTICAST MTU:1500 Metric:1
          RX packets:94207 errors:0 dropped:0 overruns:0 frame:0
          TX packets:64010 errors:0 dropped:0 overruns:0 carrier:0
          collisions:0 txqueuelen:1000
          RX bytes:125979387 (120.1 MiB) TX bytes:5853721 (5.5 MiB)
          Interrupt:22 Base address:0xde00

lo   Link encap:Local Loopback
          inet addr:127.0.0.1 Mask:255.0.0.0
          UP LOOPBACK RUNNING MTU:16436 Metric:1
          RX packets:2 errors:0 dropped:0 overruns:0 frame:0
          TX packets:2 errors:0 dropped:0 overruns:0 carrier:0
          collisions:0 txqueuelen:0
          RX bytes:100 (100.0 B) TX bytes:100 (100.0 B)

wlan0   Link encap:Ethernet HWaddr 00:1b:11:00:ac:40
          BROADCAST MULTICAST MTU:1500 Metric:1
          RX packets:0 errors:0 dropped:0 overruns:0 frame:0
          TX packets:0 errors:0 dropped:0 overruns:0 carrier:0
          collisions:0 txqueuelen:1000
          RX bytes:0 (0.0 B) TX bytes:0 (0.0 B)

175

wmaster0 Link encap:UNSPEC HWaddr 00-1B-11-00-AC-40-00-00-00-00-00-00-00-00-00-00
00-00
       BROADCAST MULTICAST MTU:1500 Metric:1
       RX packets:0 errors:0 dropped:0 overruns:0 frame:0
       TX packets:0 errors:0 dropped:0 overruns:0 carrier:0
       collisions:0 txqueuelen:1000
       RX bytes:0 (0.0 B) TX bytes:0 (0.0 B)

From the above list you can see that the computer already has an IP address
"192.168.1.64" on "eth0" therefore we need to choose a different network id,
"192.168.0.0" and make it host 1 on our ad-hoc network.

To set this and to get "wlan0" up use this.

root@slax:~# ifconfig wlan0 192.168.0.1
root@slax:~#

If all is well slax will pop up a window to say that a connection has been established to
"the_network", to check this use "ifconfig" on its own. There will also be an icon in the
right hand corner which if you roll the mouse over it will display the IP address.

root@slax:~# ifconfig
eth0   Link encap:Ethernet HWaddr 00:15:58:62:59:89
         inet addr:192.168.1.64 Bcast:192.168.1.255 Mask:255.255.255.0
         UP BROADCAST NOTRAILERS RUNNING MULTICAST MTU:1500 Metric:1
         RX packets:94315 errors:0 dropped:0 overruns:0 frame:0
         TX packets:64046 errors:0 dropped:0 overruns:0 carrier:0
         collisions:0 txqueuelen:1000
         RX bytes:125985867 (120.1 MiB) TX bytes:5855881 (5.5 MiB)
         Interrupt:22 Base address:0xde00

lo   Link encap:Local Loopback
         inet addr:127.0.0.1 Mask:255.0.0.0
         UP LOOPBACK RUNNING MTU:16436 Metric:1
         RX packets:2 errors:0 dropped:0 overruns:0 frame:0
         TX packets:2 errors:0 dropped:0 overruns:0 carrier:0
         collisions:0 txqueuelen:0
         RX bytes:100 (100.0 B) TX bytes:100 (100.0 B)

wlan0   Link encap:Ethernet HWaddr 00:1b:11:00:ac:40

inet addr:192.168.0.1 Bcast:192.168.0.255 Mask:255.255.255.0
UP BROADCAST RUNNING MULTICAST MTU:1500 Metric:1
RX packets:0 errors:0 dropped:0 overruns:0 frame:0
TX packets:0 errors:0 dropped:0 overruns:0 carrier:0
collisions:0 txqueuelen:1000
RX bytes:0 (0.0 B) TX bytes:0 (0.0 B)

wmaster0 Link encap:UNSPEC HWaddr 00-1B-11-00-AC-40-00-00-00-00-00-00-00-00-
00-00
UP BROADCAST RUNNING MULTICAST MTU:1500 Metric:1
RX packets:0 errors:0 dropped:0 overruns:0 frame:0
TX packets:0 errors:0 dropped:0 overruns:0 carrier:0
collisions:0 txqueuelen:1000
RX bytes:0 (0.0 B) TX bytes:0 (0.0 B)

We have set a static IP address here of our own choosing. The other IP address on "eth0" was given by the router that is used to connect to the internet that is known as a dynamic IP address. I am talking about the LAN IP address not the IP address that is being used to connect to the internet. On the subject of keys you can list the keys set for interfaces by using "iwlist key".

root@slax:~# iwlist key
lo   no encryption keys information.

eth0   no encryption keys information.

wmaster0 no encryption keys information.
wlan0   2 key sizes : 40, 104bits
         4 keys available :
              [1]: 6789-ABCD-EF (40 bits)
              [2]: off
              [3]: off
              [4]: off
         Current Transmit Key: [1]

There are four possible keys that can be set using the index. By the way, don't confuse this with Python. To set another key the "iwconfig" is used as follows.

root@slax:~# iwconfig wlan0 key [2] 12345678ab
root@slax:~# iwlist wlan0 key

wlan0   2 key sizes : 40, 104bits
        4 keys available :
            [1]: 6789-ABCD-EF (40 bits)
            [2]: 1234-5678-AB (40 bits)
            [3]: off
            [4]: off
        Current Transmit Key: [1]

To implement the change to the new key and to confirm do this.

root@slax:~# iwconfig wlan0 key [2]
root@slax:~# iwlist wlan0 key
wlan0   2 key sizes : 40, 104bits
        4 keys available :
            [1]: 6789-ABCD-EF (40 bits)
            [2]: 1234-5678-AB (40 bits)
            [3]: off
            [4]: off
        Current Transmit Key: [2]

wlan0   IEEE 802.11bg ESSID:"the_network"
        Mode:Ad-Hoc Frequency:2.412 GHz Cell: Not-Associated
        Tx-Power=13 dBm
        Retry min limit:7 RTS thr:off Fragment thr=2352 B
        Encryption key:1234-5678-AB [2]
        Power Management:off
        Link Quality:0 Signal level:0 Noise level:0
        Rx invalid nwid:0 Rx invalid crypt:0 Rx invalid frag:0
        Tx excessive retries:0 Invalid misc:0   Missed beacon:0

Now to set up the other computer it is exactly the same if you are using another copy of the downloadable CD.
Here on the lap top the interface is "eth2".
root@slax:~# iwlist scanning
lo   Interface doesn't support scanning.

eth1   Interface doesn't support scanning.

eth2   Scan completed :
        Cell 01 - Address: 46:62:7A:BD:74:93

ESSID:"the_network"
Protocol:IEEE 802.11bg
Mode:Ad-Hoc
Frequency:2.412 GHz (Channel 1)
Encryption key:on
Bit Rates:1 Mb/s; 2 Mb/s; 5.5 Mb/s; 11 Mb/s; 6 Mb/s
    9 Mb/s; 12 Mb/s; 18 Mb/s; 24 Mb/s; 36 Mb/s
    48 Mb/s; 54 Mb/s
Quality=91/100 Signal level=-38 dBm
Extra: Last beacon: 76ms ago
Cell 02 - Address: 00:18:F6:AC:3F:41
ESSID:"BTHomeHub-C76A"
Protocol:IEEE 802.11bg
Mode:Master
Frequency:2.442 GHz (Channel 7)
Encryption key:on
Bit Rates:1 Mb/s; 2 Mb/s; 5.5 Mb/s; 6 Mb/s; 9 Mb/s
    11 Mb/s; 12 Mb/s; 18 Mb/s; 24 Mb/s; 36 Mb/s
    48 Mb/s; 54 Mb/s
Quality=95/100 Signal level=-31 dBm
Extra: Last beacon: 244ms ago

Setting up "eth2"

root@slax:~# ifconfig eth2 down

root@slax:~# iwconfig eth2 essid the_network mode ad-hoc key 12345678ab

Checking the setup.

root@slax:~# iwconfig
lo   no wireless extensions.

eth1   no wireless extensions.

eth2   IEEE 802.11g ESSID:"the_network"
      Mode:Ad-Hoc Frequency:2.412 GHz Cell: 46:62:7A:BD:74:93
      Bit Rate:54 Mb/s Tx-Power=20 dBm Sensitivity=8/0

Retry limit:7 RTS thr:off Fragment thr:off
Encryption key:1234-5678-AB Security mode:open
Power Management:off
Link Quality=71/100 Signal level=-57 dBm Noise level=-85 dBm
Rx invalid nwid:0 Rx invalid crypt:0 Rx invalid frag:0
Tx excessive retries:0 Invalid misc:0 Missed beacon:0

Setting the IP address and getting the interface up, note same network id, different host.

root@slax:~# ifconfig eth2 192.168.0.2

                                                                root@slax:~#

Now if your browser, say Firefox, is opened on the second computer and "192.168.0.1" entered in the URL address box the modified message from the first computer should be visible.

8.5 Using Your Home Network

If you have a wireless router you can make use of your home LAN.

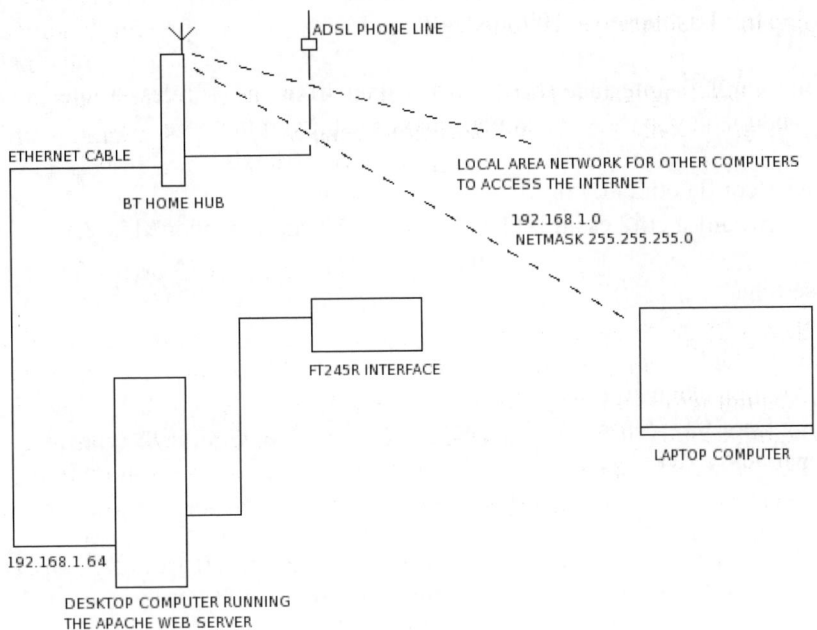

Firstly if the first computer is plugged in to the router when it boots up it will connect automatically. Setting up the second computer for Wi-Fi is similar to the ad-hoc network except that you have to use the network name, key and IP address that is given.

root@slax:~# iwlist scanning
lo   Interface doesn't support scanning.

eth1   Interface doesn't support scanning.

eth2   Scan completed :
      Cell 01 - Address: 00:18:F6:AC:3F:41
          ESSID:"BTHomeHub-C76A"
          Protocol:IEEE 802.11bg
          Mode:Master
          Frequency:2.442 GHz (Channel 7)

Encryption key:on
Bit Rates:1 Mb/s; 2 Mb/s; 5.5 Mb/s; 6 Mb/s; 9 Mb/s
    11 Mb/s; 12 Mb/s; 18 Mb/s; 24 Mb/s; 36 Mb/s
    48 Mb/s; 54 Mb/s
Quality=94/100 Signal level=-33 dBm
Extra: Last beacon: 1096ms ago

To set up the wireless interface the essid is taken from the wireless router, the mode is "managed" and the key is for your router, I haven't stated mine here.

root@slax:~# ifconfig eth2 down
root@slax:~# iwconfig eth2 essid BTHomeHub-C76A mode managed key a_____b

Check the settings.

root@slax:~# iwconfig
lo   no wireless extensions.

eth1   no wireless extensions.

eth2   IEEE 802.11g ESSID:"BTHomeHub-C76A"
       Mode:Managed Frequency:2.442 GHz Access Point: 00:18:F6:AC:3F:41
       Bit Rate:54 Mb/s   Tx-Power=20 dBm   Sensitivity=8/0
       Retry limit:7 RTS thr:off Fragment thr:off
       Encryption key:A____-____-_B Security mode:open
       Power Management:off
       Link Quality=89/100 Signal level=-40 dBm Noise level=-88 dBm
       Rx invalid nwid:0 Rx invalid crypt:0 Rx invalid frag:0
       Tx excessive retries:0 Invalid misc:6   Missed beacon:5

Last of all the IP address is obtained by using the command "dhcpcd", if all goes well you will be connected.

root@slax:~# dhcpcd eth2
Broadcasting DHCP_DISCOVER
broadcastAddr option is missing in DHCP server response. Assuming 192.168.1.255
dhcpIPaddrLeaseTime=86400 in DHCP server response.
dhcpT1value is missing in DHCP server response. Assuming 43200 sec
dhcpT2value is missing in DHCP server response. Assuming 75600 sec
DHCP_OFFER received from (192.168.1.254)

Broadcasting DHCP_REQUEST for 192.168.1.71
dhcpIPaddrLeaseTime=86400 in DHCP server response.
dhcpT1value is missing in DHCP server response. Assuming 43200 sec
dhcpT2value is missing in DHCP server response. Assuming 75600 sec
DHCP_ACK received from (192.168.1.254)
Broadcasting ARPOP_REQUEST for 192.168.1.71
root@slax~#

To access the server you need go to the other computer and either mouse over the icon in the corner or use "ifconfig". In chapter 11 there will be a workaround for the problem you might notice with rendering graphics using Firefox 3.5.6 with Linux.

8.6 The Apache Folders

To keep things simple all the files that are to be written will be in the folders under "/usr/local/apache2", this means that any changes will have to saved to a flash drive before shutdown and copied back up after the next reboot but this can be automated. Using the files in this location has the advantage that when a project is finished a new customized CD can be burned with the application on it. This will be done in chapter 11.

Chapter 9

Write a simple Web Site

9.1 Introduction

This chapter will be about html and producing simple web pages. The pages will not be interfacing with the hardware boards. A basic knowledge of html will be needed because in the next chapter Python code running on the server will be writing html on the fly to produce pages that do interface with hardware. In order to produce a graphic user interface to the hardware we need only the simplest of web pages.

9.2 The Apache File system

Fig. 9 – 1 shows the directory tree under the "/usr/local/apache2/" directory.

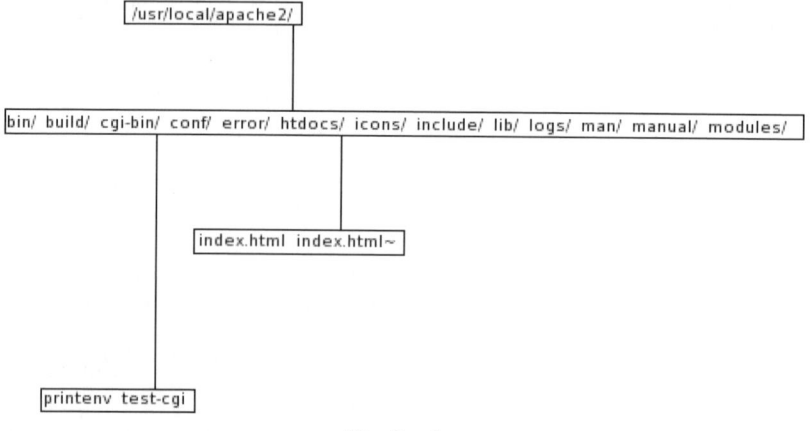

Fig 9 - 1

The home page and other pages and files such as images will be in the "htdocs" directory and subdirectories that have yet to be created. The Python code in the next chapter will be in "cgi-bin" directory, this stands for common gateway interface binary files. Other languages can be used for writing CGI files.

All you need to write a web page is a text editor, you can view the page directly by navigating to the html file, with a web browser, "konqueror" and Firefox are on the CD.

184

This won't work for webpages that call on server side code therefore all the examples will be described by viewing them using apache. When apache runs web pages can be viewed on the IP address "127.0.0.1" which is called "localhost" this was demonstrated in the previous chapter, this gives a convenient way of testing a web site before putting it on a LAN or the internet.

In order to make it easier all of the examples are on the CD and a sub-directory tree for each example is there under "/root/programs/chap09_progs/" and "/root/programs/chap09_progs/". For the first example carry out the following.

```
root@slax:~# cd /root/programs/chap09_progs/prog01/
root@slax:~/programs/chap09_progs/prog01# ls
htdocs/
root@slax:~/programs/chap09_progs/prog01# cp -r htdocs/ /usr/local/apache2/
root@slax:~/programs/chap09_progs/prog01#
```

You copy the entire directory "htdocs" by using the option "-r" which means recursively to the apache server.

9.3 Hyper Text Makeup Language

HTML documents are made up of elements that are blocks enclosed by tags. Tags are enclosed by "<>" brackets, there is an opening tag to an element and usually a closing tag, some elements do not have a closing tag, examples will make this clear. The first tag is "<html>" which marks the start of the html document the last tag is </html> which marks the end of the html, note the "/" in front of html this tells the browser it is a closing tag. The short document below, Prog 9 – 1 is a trivial web page that demonstrates how opening and closing tags work. The "<head>...<./head> tags contain the "<title>.....</title> tags which contain the test that will appear in the browser's title bar. This nesting of elements is the main principle to understand with html. The "<br>" tag is the line break and is one of the empty elements that do not have a closing tag. Simply typing a newline in the source code will not appear as a newline on the web page you have to use the "<br>" tag. Prog 9 - 1 is file "index.html" which is the file that apache is configured to display when only the server root is given as the address.

```
<html>
<head>
<title>Example Home Page</title>
```

```
</head>
<body>
<h1>This is a heading</h1>
<h2>This is a smaller heading</h2>
<h1>This is another big heading<h1>
<h3>This is very small heading</h3>
This is a line of text.<br>This is another line of text.<br>
<u>This line is underlined.</u>
</body>
</html>
```

Prog 9 – 1

For the purpose of interfacing with our hardware we only need a limited html repertoire. Placing images on the page is going to be used for instrumentation, the techniques described in chapter 5 will be used to manipulate bitmap images. Prog 9 – 2 places an image with the "<img>" tag. This is another empty element that has no closing tag. The attribute of the tag is the path to the image file on the server. A directory "images" in the "http" directory was created to hold images.

```
<html>
<head>
<title>Example Home Page</title>
</head>
<body style="background-color:#c0c0c0">
<p style="color:#ffffff">Image One</p>
<img src="images/image1.jpg">
<p>Back to black</p><br><br>
</body>
</html>
```

Prog 9 – 2

To see this page in the browser copy the "htdocs" directory recursively as shown here.

```
root@slax:~# cd /root/programs/chap09_progs/prog_09_02/
root@slax:~/programs/chap09_progs/prog_09_02# ls
htdocs/
root@slax:~/programs/chap09_progs/prog_09_02# cp -r htdocs/ /usr/local/apache2/
root@slax:~/programs/chap09_progs/prog_09_02#
```

Reload "http://localhost" in the browser and the web page should appear. In the body tag the style attribute has been added to change the background colour to grey. One line has been added to include a one line paragraph with the tags "<p> ....</p>" and the style attribute setting the text for this paragraph to white. The style change is limited to this paragraph. The paragraph after the image is the default colour as there is no style set for it.

The use of in-line style setting is not the recommended way of doing it for more complicated web sites. For extremely simple pages like these the alternative methods of internal or external style sheets where the aim is to separate style and content is not justified and won't be dealt with here.

9.4 Table Layout

The table layout method will be used to place images and text on the page, as it gives reliable results and is easy to implement. It is also similar to Tkinter's "grid" layout method.

```
<html>
<head>
<title>Example Home Page</title>
</head>
<body style="background-color:#c0c0c0">
<table>
<tr><td><img                src="images/image1.jpg"></td><td           rowspan="2"><img
src="images/image3.jpg"><td></tr>
<tr><td><img src="images/image2.jpg"></td></tr>
</table>
</body>
</html>
```

      Prog 9 – 3

The table is between the "<table>.....</table> tags. Each row of the table is between "<tr>....</tr>" table row tags, and each cell of the table is between "<td>....</td> table data tags. Fig. 9 – 2 shows how this appears, "image 3" is in the top row and the right column but spans two rows. The bottom row has "image2" in the left cell.

For this example copy recursively the "htdocs" directory from.

187

"root/programs/chap09_progs/prog_09_03/" to "/usr/local/apache2/".

```
root@slax:~# cd /root/programs/chap09_progs/prog_09_03/
root@slax:~/programs/chap09_progs/prog_09_03# ls
htdocs/
root@slax:~/programs/chap09_progs/prog_09_03# cp -r htdocs/ /usr/local/apache2/
root@slax:~/programs/chap09_progs/prog_09_03#
```

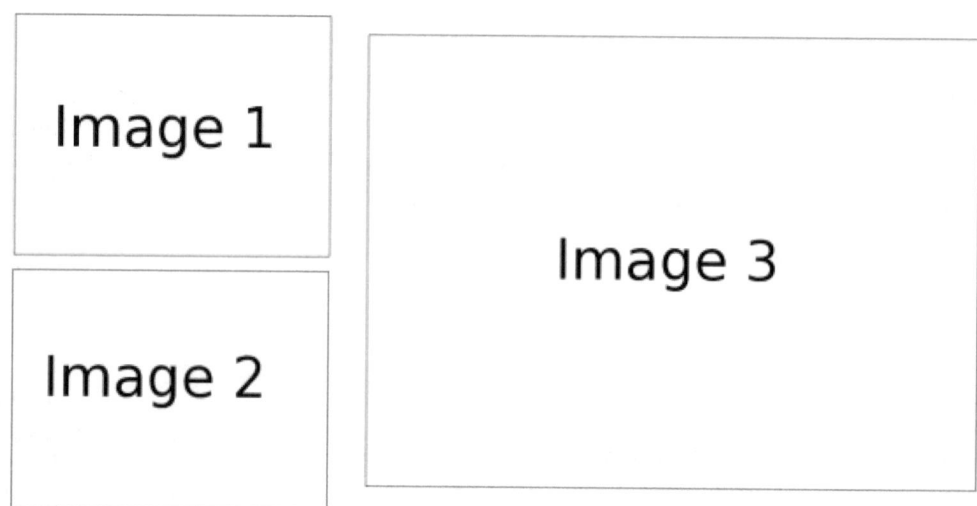

Fig 9 - 2

9.5 The URL

To go to a web site you have to enter a uniform resource locator URL in the address bar of the browser. To go to our apache web server on the same computer the URL is "http://localhost" or "http://127.0.0.1". The URL is made up of the protocol "http:/" and the domain "/localhost", following on from the domain can be a path and a file name. If there is no path and file name then the server will return "index.html" from the "htdocs' directory.

Most web sites have more than one page, it is a way of keeping related material in one place, by using hyperlinks it is easy for the user to jump from page to page or to other sites. A website that is used as an interface to a control system could have different instruments and controls on different pages. Prog 9 – 4 is made up of a "home page" and "page2".

```
<html>
<head>
<title>Example Home Page</title>
</head>
<body style="background-color:#c0c0c0">
<a href="page2.html" style="color:#ffff00">LINK TO PAGE 2</a>
</body>
</html>
```

Prog 9 – 4 - Part 1 (index.html)

The "<a>.....</a>" tags enclose the hyperlink to "page2". As "page2.html" is in the same directory as "index.html" only the file name is required in the URL. On "page2" are two other links, one is back to the home page and one is to the Elektor Website.

```
<html>
<head>
<title>Page 2</title>
</head>
<body style="background-color:#0000">
<h1 style="colour:#ffffff"">WELCOME TO PAGE 2</h1>
<a href="index.html">Home</a>
 
<a href=http://www.elektor.com>The Elektor Website</a>
</body>
</html>
```

Prog 9 – 4 - Part 2 (page2.html)

For this example copy recursively the "htdocs" directory from "root/programs/chap09_progs/prog_09_04/" to "/usr/local/apache2/".

```
root@slax:~# cd /root/programs/chap09_progs/prog_09_04/
root@slax:~/programs/chap09_progs/prog_09_04# ls
htdocs/
root@slax:~/programs/chap09_progs/prog_09_04# cp -r htdocs/ /usr/local/apache2/
```

189

9.6 Forms

In order to pass information from the client to the server so that control of hardware can be achieved we need a mechanism to input data and send it. Forms provide a way of doing this. The data that is sent to the server is used by a program in the "/usr/local/apache2/cgi-bin" directory. Writing programs to go into this directory will be the subject of chapter 10. In order to demonstrate how to write forms a Python program "demo-cgi.py" has been provided here without explanation. This program simply returns the inputted data to the client's screen on a different page.

```
<html>
<head>
<title>Example Home Page</title>
</head>
<body>
<form action = "/cgi-bin/demo_cgi.py"  method="post">
<input type="checkbox" name="One" value="on">I</input>
<input type="checkbox" name="Two" value="on">II</input>
<input type="checkbox" name="Three" value="on">III</input>
<input type="checkbox" name="Four" value="on" checked>IV</input>
<input type="checkbox" name="Five" value="on">V</input>
<input type="checkbox" name="Six" value="on">VI</input>
<br><br>
<input type='radio' name="letters" value="a">A</input>
<input type='radio' name="letters" value="b">B</input>
<input type='radio' name="letters" value="c" checked>C</input>
<input type='radio' name="letters" value="d" checked>D</input>
<input type='radio' name="letters" value="e">E</input>
<input type='radio' name="letters" value="f" >F</input>
<br><br>
<input type="text" name="user_input" value="hhmmss" ></input>Set Timer
<br><br>
<input type="password" name="pass">Password</input>
<br><br>
<select name="voltage">
<option value="5">+5</option>
<option value="10">+10</option>
<option value="15">+15</option>
```

```
<option value="24">+24</option>
<option value="30">+30</option>
</select>Voltage
<br><br><br>
<input type="submit" value="SEND TO THE CGI PROGRAM"></input>
</form>
</body>
</html>
```

Prog 9 – 5

The form is enclosed in the "<form>......</form>" tags. There are two attributes belonging to this form. The first is "action" which is the path and the file name of the CGI program that is going to handle the form on the server, the second attribute is the "method" in this case "post". There are two methods available; "get" and "post". We will only be using "post" as this is the method recommended for actions that have the effect of making changes as opposed to just retrieving data. The first six input widgets are check boxes, when the data ends up being handled by the Python program it will be as a dictionary, the names of the checkboxes will be the keys and the value given to each checkbox will be the value in the dictionary for that key. In this program box "Four" is pre-checked by adding the attribute "checked". After each widget there is some plain text to describe the use to the user. Next there are six radio buttons.They are all given the name "letters" to make them into a group, you can have more than one group of radio buttons in a form by giving each group a distinct name for its buttons. Again one of the buttons is pre-checked. There is a "textbox" whose name here is "user_input", a default entry can be given using the "value" attribute. There is a password box. This only gives a very low level of security as the password is transmitted in plain text and could be read by anyone who can monitor the network traffic. The last data input widget is a drop down menu that is enclosed by the "<select>.....</select>" tags and contains "<option>....</option>" tags.

In order to send the data an input type "submit" creates a button with the "value" setting the button text.

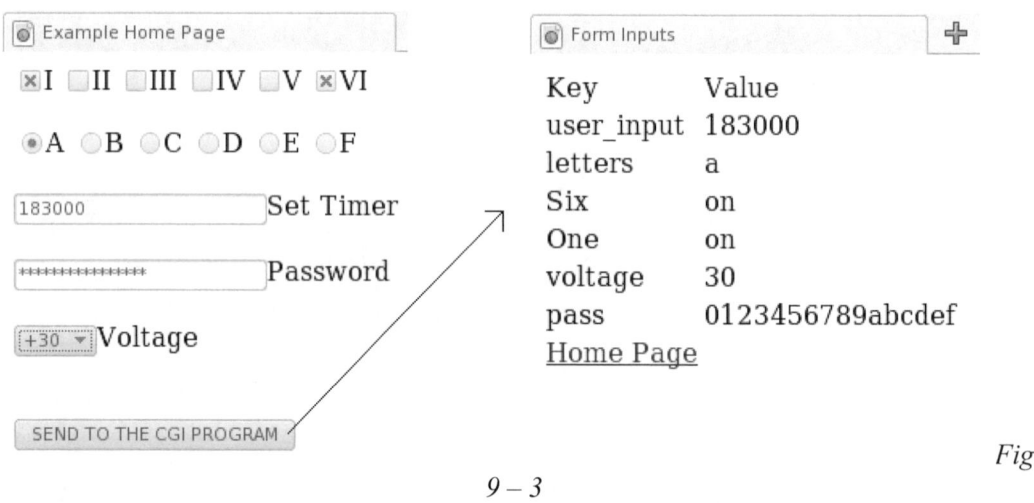

Fig
9 – 3

Fig 9 – 3 shows the home page on the left as the form appears with some entries made, and on the right is the returned page when the submit button is pressed. When used for control

192

purposes the CGI program will communicate with another program that will be interfacing with the hardware. Note that a dictionary is not in any predictable order, its members are indexed by key so this does not matter.

For this example copy recursively the "htdocs" and "cgi-bin directories from "root/programs/chap09_progs/prog_09_05/" to "/usr/local/apache2/".

```
root@slax:~# cd /root/programs/chap09_progs/prog_09_05/
root@slax:~/programs/chap09_progs/prog_09_05# ls
htdocs/   cgi-bin/
root@slax:~/programs/chap09_progs/prog_09_05#   cp   -r   htdocs/   cgi-bin/
/usr/local/apache2/
root@slax:~/programs/chap09_progs/prog_09_05#
```

Chapter 10

Server Side Code

10.1 Introduction

In this chapter we are going to write code that runs on the server and handles the input from the forms. What goes on here can be quite difficult to understand. The CGI program is a Python program but its print statements do not print to the screen. Instead, they print to a file which will be the html that is sent to the client. As well as doing this the CGI program can do all the other things that a Python program can do including reading and writing other files on the local computer.

10.2 Common Gateway Interface

The last chapter dealt with forms and inputting data into a web page. In the example given the form was on the home page and the CGI program generated a page displaying the inputted data. The next example, Prog 10 – 1, will have a home page with a link to a CGI program, the CGI program will generate a web page with a form on it, submitting this form will then call the same cgi file again. To run this program you need to copy directories recursively, preserving permissions, to the server as shown below, using the "-rp" options. The three directories are "htdocs/", "cgi-bin/", and "ftdi_bin".

```
root@slax:~# cd programs/chap10_progs/prog_10_01/
root@slax:~/programs/chap10_progs/prog_10_01# ls
cgi-bin/  ftdi_bin/  htdocs/
root@slax:~/programs/chap10_progs/prog_10_01# cp -rp * /usr/local/apache2/
root@slax:~/programs/chap10_progs/prog_10_01#
```

```
<html>
<head><title>Home Page</title></head>
<body>
<a href="/cgi-bin/10_01_cgi.py"><img src="images/button1.png"></img></a>
</body>
</html>
```

Prog 10 – 1 Part 1 (index.html)

194

Prog 10 - 1 Part 1 is the home page. Instead of a text link there is an image that is being used as a link. By including an image you can create your own customized buttons. Clicking on this image calls the CGI program "/usr/local/apache2/10_01_cgi.py", you only have to start the path at "/cgi-bin/" as the server has been configured to look from here for CGI files.

Prog 10 – 1 Part 2 is the CGI program. Up until now all our Python programs have been run from the command line by typing "python program_name.py". In looking at the first line of the CGI program what looks like a comment is actually an instruction to the operating system to run Python. For this to work the file has to be made executable and readable by others by using "chmod 755 10_01_cgi.py".
The module that needs to be imported to make it work as a CGI program is the "CGI" module; this is what handles the form dictionaries. The line "form=cgi.FieldStorage()" creates the instance of the class that handles the form input.

One problem with writing CGI programs is, if you make a mistake and the program crashes, then because the print statements are not written to the screen you won't see any error messages. To get round this you import the "sys" module, then the line "sys.stderr = sys.stdout" directs error so that they appear on the web page.

In order for your printed output to form an html document for the client the line "print Content-type:text/html" followed by at least one blank line must start the html. It is best to put this in front of all the rest of the program so that any mistakes that get caught appear on the screen. If you are faced with an internal server error, there may be other clues if you open the "/usr/local/logs/error_log" with the text editor.


```
#!/usr/local/bin/python
import cgi,time,os
import sys, time, pickle

sys.stderr = sys.stdout
form = cgi.FieldStorage()

print 'Content-type: text/html'
print

time_stamp_ = 0
output5_ = 'OFF'
message="
status_ =-1
```

```python
if form.has_key('DB5'):
    cgi2output_dict = {}

    cgi2output_dict['output5_command'] = form['DB5'].value
    f=open('../ftdi_bin/cgi2output','w')
    pickle.dump(cgi2output_dict, f)
    f.close()

try:
    f=open('../ftdi_bin/output2cgi','r')
    output2cgi_dict=pickle.load(f)
    f.close()

    time_stamp_ = output2cgi_dict['time_stamp']
    output5_ = output2cgi_dict['output5_state']
    status_ = message=output2cgi_dict['status']
    if status_ == 0:
        message ='<p style="color:#ffffff">HEALTHY</p>'

    else:
        message ='<p style="color:#ff0000">DEVICE MISSING</p>'
except:
    pass

if time.time()- time_stamp_ > 10:
    message='<p style = "color:#ff0000">CONTROLLER NOT RUNNING</p>'


print '<head><title>Outputs Over the Network  </title></head>'
print '<body bgcolor="#808080">'
print '<form action="../cgi-bin/output_cgi.py" method="post">'
print'<input type="submit" name="DB5" value = "OFF"/></form>'
print '<form action="../cgi-bin/output_cgi.py" method="post">'
print '<input type="submit" name="DB5" value = "ON"/></form><br><br>'
print '<form action="../cgi-bin/output_cgi.py" method="post">'
print '<input type="submit"  value="READ OUTPUT"/></form><br><br>'
if output5_ =='OFF':
    print '<img src="../images/lamp_off.png"></img><br><br>'
else:
    print '<img src = "../images/lamp_on.png"></img><br><br>'
print message
print '</body>'
```

Prog 10 – 1 Part 2 (10_01_cgi.py)

When the CGI program is called from the home page there is no form input data. When the "submit" button is pressed the CGI program is called again but this time there will be form data from the radio buttons. The program checks to see if the "switch" key is there and then reads its value. This value is used to write "ON" or "OFF" to the screen and to log it to the file "usr/local/apache/ftdi_bin/switch_log.csv". This can be read with a spread sheet program. Fig 10 – 1 gives an overview of what is happening.

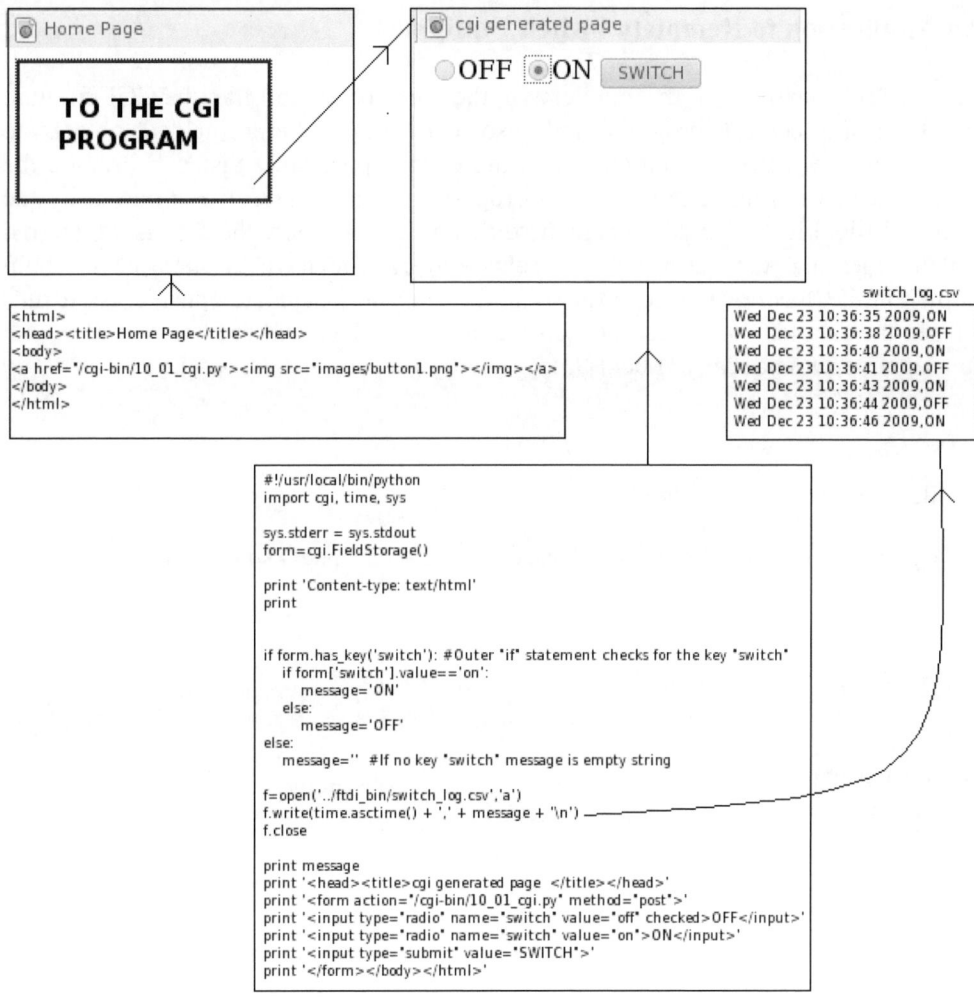

Fig 10 – 1

197

As the purpose of all this to control or monitor hardware there has to be communication with another program that is interfacing with that hardware. This other program will be running all of the time and data will be passed between the CGI program when it runs and the control program by way of intermediate data files. The next program, Prog 10 – 2, is a simple application where digital outputs can be turned on and off remotely.

10.3 An Application to Remotely Switch Equipment

There are five files involved in this application, the home page html file, the CGI program file, the hardware control program and also two files holding pickled objects to communicate between the CGI program and the control program. Listed below are the "index.html" which is similar to the one in Prog 10 – 1, then the CGI file and lastly the output control file. Fig 10 – 2 is a schematic diagram showing how the data is transferred between the files and the hardware. To make it work you have to start the program "output.py" on the "/usr/local/apache/ftdi_bin" directory in a separate console. As it runs you will see the data that is passed between the programs. The next chapter will deal with starting programs automatically at boot time.

```
<html>
<head><title>Home Page</title></head>
<body>
<a href="/cgi-bin/output_cgi.py"><img src="images/button_output.png"></img></a>
</body>
</html>
```

Prog 10 – 2 Part 1 (index.html)

```
#!/usr/local/bin/python
import cgi,time,os
import sys, time, pickle

sys.stderr = sys.stdout
form = cgi.FieldStorage()

print 'Content-type: text/html'
print

time_stamp_ = 0
output5_  = 'OFF'
```

```python
message="
status_=-1
if form.has_key('DB5'):
    cgi2output_dict = {}

    cgi2output_dict['output5_command'] = form['DB5'].value
    f=open('../ftdi_bin/cgi2output','w')
    pickle.dump(cgi2output_dict, f)
    f.close()

try:
    f=open('../ftdi_bin/output2cgi','r')
    output2cgi_dict=pickle.load(f)
    f.close()

    time_stamp_ = output2cgi_dict['time_stamp']
    output5_ = output2cgi_dict['output5_state']
    status_ = message=output2cgi_dict['status']
    if status_ == 0:
        message ='<p style="color:#ffffff">HEALTHY</p>'

    else:
        message ='<p style="color:#ff0000">DEVICE MISSING</p>'
except:
    pass

if time.time()- time_stamp_ > 10:
    message='<p style = "color:#ff0000">CONTROLLER NOT RUNNING</p>'



print '<head><title>Outputs Over the Network  </title></head>'
print '<body bgcolor="#808080">'
print '<form action="../cgi-bin/output_cgi.py" method="post">'
print'<input type="submit" name="DB5" value = "OFF"/></form>'
print '<form action="../cgi-bin/output_cgi.py" method="post">'
print '<input type="submit" name="DB5" value = "ON"/></form><br><br>'
print '<form action="../cgi-bin/output_cgi.py" method="post">'
print '<input type="submit"  value="READ OUTPUT"/></form><br><br>'
if output5_ =='OFF':
    print '<img src="../images/lamp_off.png"></img><br><br>'
else:
    print '<img src = "../images/lamp_on.png"></img><br><br>'
print message
```

199

print '</body>'

```python
#!/usr/local/bin/python
from interface_classes import *
import pickle, time

dev1=DeviceB('FTCVMOYU')
output2cgi_dict = {}
cgi2output_dict = {}
db5 = 'OFF'

while 1:

    dev1.ads1286()  #Just to generate CS pulses for the watchdog monostable.
    a = dev1.data1    #To check for device still present

    try:

        f = open('cgi2output','r')

        cgi2output_dict=pickle.load(f)
        f.close()
        if cgi2output_dict['output5_command']=='ON':
            db5 = 'ON'
            dev1.pin_on(32)  # DB5  binary weighting
        else:
            db5 = 'OFF'
            dev1.pin_off(32)
    except:
        pass

    if a < 0:
        output2cgi_dict['status']=-1
    else:
        output2cgi_dict['status']=0

    output2cgi_dict['time_stamp']=time.time()
    output2cgi_dict['output5_state']=db5
```

200

```
f=open('output2cgi','w')
pickle.dump(output2cgi_dict,f)
f.close()
print 'output2cgi_dict', output2cgi_dict
print 'cgi2output_dict', cgi2output_dict
print
```
Prog 10 – 2 Part 3 (output.py)

The explanation will begin by dealing with the control file "output.py", this file is in the directory "/usr/local/apache2/ftdi_bin". An instance of the class "DeviceB" provides the interface with a circuit as shown in Fig 7 – 5. The program in this file sets an output on or off according to commands from the CGI file. These commands are transmitted by the CGI file writing to the file "cgi2output" in the "ftdi_bin" directory, the control file is running a continous loop that is reading this file for new commands. The control file also writes to a file "output2cgi" which is read by the CGI file when it runs. This way data is passed in both directions between the CGI file and the control file. The data that is transmitted is in the form of dictionaries.

The dictionary transmitted through "cgi2ouput" and read by "output.py" is "cgi2output_dict" and has key, "output5_command" it has only one member here but could have up to three if all the outputs on a "DeviceB" board were used. The data is pickled and unpickled for transmission through the file.

In the other direction the dictionary through the "output2cgi" file is "output2cgi_dict" and has keys "status" which tells if the device is still plugged in, "time_stamp" that is used by the CGI program to determine if the control program is still running, and "output5_state" that tells the last state of the output. Although there are no analog inputs being used the "ads1286()" function is being called to produce pulses for the watchdog monostable which will inhibit the opto-coupler in the event of the program stopping. Also the value of "dev1.data0" is being checked as this will be negative if the device is unplugged, this is what determines the status value in the dictionary.

The CGI program is initially called by a user clicking on the button on the home page. The CGI page then appears on the web browser and the user can click on the "ON" or "OFF" buttons. This sets the value of the "DB5" key and runs the CGI program again, this time the new value of "DB5" is used to set the "output5_command" in the "cgi2output_dict" dictionary and on to the control program "output.py".

The CGI program also checks to see if the time_stamp is older than 10 seconds since if so the controller is no longer running. Also if the "status" key value is negative the device is unplugged. Looking at the source code above it should be apparent how this all works.

The user has to call for updates by using the "READ OUTPUT" button.

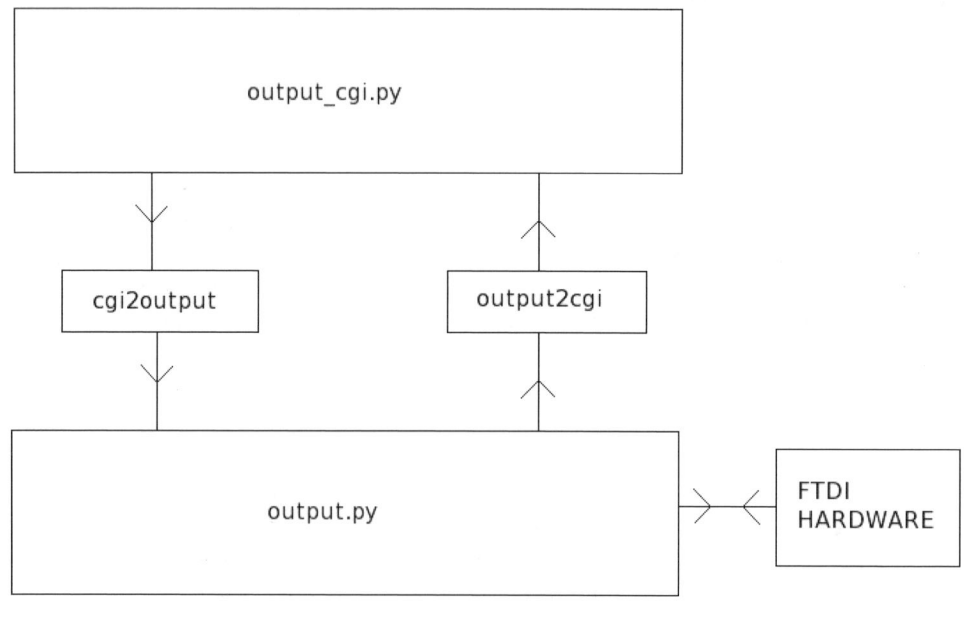

Fig 10 – 2

The data being transferred between files can be viewed in the console window where "/usr/local/apache2/ftdi_bin/output.py" is running. Below is an example

output2cgi_dict {'status': 0, 'time_stamp': 1262253272.3588409, 'output5_state': 'ON'}
cgi2output_dict {'output5_command': 'ON'}

10.4 Remote Temperature Controller

The last project is the most complicated in the book and makes use of the bitmap manipulation from chapter 5 to draw a temperature instrument as part of a controller with remotely adjustable setpoint and hysteresis. Everything in this program has been covered before and it is left to the reader to look at the code to understand in detail how it works. There is a mimic of a thermometer that gets drawn according to the temperature, with marks to indicate the setpoint and hysteresis. The user can enable or disable the control and change the setpoint and hysteresis. Like the output control above, the user can see if the control program is still running or if the hardware has failed or been unplugged. There are four scripts involved and two files to transmit data. There is the home page "index.html" there are two CGI programs "display_cgi.py" and "configure_cgi.py" and there is the "controller_cgi.py" in the "/usr/local/apache/ftdi" directory that has to be started manually.

```
<html>
<head>
<title>Networked Temperature Controller</title>
</head>
<body bgcolor="#808080">
<form action="../cgi-bin/display_cgi.py" method="get">
<img  src="images/home.png"></img><br><br>
<input type="submit" name="read" value="CHANNEL 1">
</form>
</body>
</html>
```

Prog 10 – 3 Part 1 (index.html)

```
#!/usr/local/bin/python
import cgi,time,os
import sys
import time
import pickle

sys.stderr = sys.stdout
form=cgi.FieldStorage()
print 'Content-type: text/html'
print
drive_col = '#000000'
enabled_col = '#000000'
time_stamp_ = 0
warning_flag = True
try:
    cgi2cont_cx = {}
    if form.has_key('commit'):
        if form['commit'].value == 'yes':
            cgi2cont_cx['setpoint'] = form['setpoint'].value
            cgi2cont_cx['hysteresis'] = form['hysteresis'].value
            f=open('../ftdi_bin/cgi2cont','w')
            pickle.dump(cgi2cont_cx, f)
```

203

```python
            f.close()

    if form.has_key('commit2'):
      if form['commit2'].value == 'yes':
        if form['enable'].value == 'on':
          cgi2cont_cx['enable'] = True
        else:
          cgi2cont_cx['enable'] = False
        f=open('../ftdi_bin/cgi2cont','w')
        pickle.dump(cgi2cont_cx, f)
        f.close()
except:
  pass
try:
  f=open('../ftdi_bin/cont2cgi','r')
  cont2cgi_dict=pickle.load(f)
  f.close()
  status_=cont2cgi_dict['status']
  enabled_=cont2cgi_dict['enabled']
  drive_on_=cont2cgi_dict['drive_on']
  time_stamp_=cont2cgi_dict['time_stamp']
  if status_==0:
    message="HEALTHY"
    mess_col='#ffffff'
    warning_flag=False
  else:
    message="DEVICE MISSING"
    mess_col='#ff0000'
    warning_flag = True

  if drive_on_:
    drive_col = '#00ff00'
  else:
    drive_col = '#ff0000'

  if enabled_:
    enabled_col = '#00ff00'
  else:
    enabled_col = '#ff0000'
except:
  pass

if time.time() - time_stamp_ > 20:
  message='CONTROLLER NOT RUNNING'
```

```python
    mess_col = '#ff0000'
    warning_flag = True

print '<html><head><title>Networked Temperature Controller</title>'
print '</head><body style = "background:#808080">'
print '<form action = "../cgi-bin/configure_cgi.py" method = "post">'
print '<table>'
if warning_flag:
    print '<tr><td rowspan = 5><img src="../images/display1_warn.bmp" ></img></td>'
else:
    print '<tr><td rowspan=5><img src="../images/display1.bmp" ></img></td>'

print '<td style="color:' + mess_col + '">' + message + '</td></tr>'
print '<tr><td style="color:' + enabled_col + '">ENABLED</td></tr>'
print '<tr><td style="color:' + drive_col + '">DRIVE</td></tr></td>'
print '<tr><td><input type="submit" value="CONFIGURE"></td></tr></form>'
print '<form action="../cgi-bin/display_cgi.py" method="post"><tr><td>'
print '<input type="submit" value="UPDATE"><tr></form>'
print '<tr><td><a href = "../index.html"style="color:black">HOME</a></td></tr></form>'
print '</table>'
```

Prog 10 – 3 Part 2 (display_cgi.py)

```
#!/usr/local/bin/python
import cgi,time,os
import sys
import time
import pickle

sys.stderr = sys.stdout
form=cgi.FieldStorage()

#HTML sent to the client
print 'Content-type: text/html'
print
print
print '<head><title>Networked Temperature Controller</title></head>'
print '<body bgcolor = "#808080">'

print '<form action="../cgi-bin/display_cgi.py" method="post">'
print '<table>'
print '<tr><td>SETPOINT</td><td>HYSTERESIS</td></tr>'
print '<tr><td><select name = "setpoint">'
for n in range (-5,45):
    sn=str(n)
    print '<option value=' + sn + '>'+ sn +'</option>'
print '</select></td>'
print '<td><select name = "hysteresis">'
for n in range (0,5):
    sn=str(n)
    print '<option value =' + sn + '>'+ sn +'</option>'
print '</select></td></tr>'
print '<tr><td><input type="checkbox" name="commit" value="yes"/>COMMIT</td></tr>'
print '<tr><td><input type="submit" value="RETURN"></input><td></tr>'
print '</table></form></body></html>'
print '<br>_____<br><br>'
print '<form action="../cgi-bin/display_cgi.py" method="get">'
print '<table>'
print '<tr><td><input type = "radio" name = "enable" value = "on"/>ENABLE</td></tr>'
print '<tr><td><input type = "radio" name = "enable" value = "off"/>DISABLE</td></tr>'
print '<tr><td><input type = "checkbox" name = "commit2" value = "yes"/>COMMIT</td></tr>'
print '<tr><td><input type = "submit" value = "RETURN"></input></td></tr>'
print '</table></form></body></html>'
print '</table>'
print '</body>'
```

Prog 10 – 3 Part 3 (configure_cgi.py)

```python
#!/usr/local/bin/python
from interface_classes import *
import pickle
from time import *
import os
from bmp_draw import *

class Cont():
    def __init__(self,devices):
        self.devices = devices
        self.enable_flag = False
        self.temperature = 0
        self.m = 0.033364
        self.c = -27.877019
        self.cgi2cont_dict = {'setpoint':'20','hysteresis':'1','enable':False}
        self.cont2cgi_dict = {'enabled':False,'drive_on':False, 'status':0}

    def read_temp(self):
        raw_total = 0
        for n in range(0,20):
            self.devices[0].ads1286()
            raw=self.devices[0].data0
            raw_total = raw + raw_total

        raw_average = raw_total/20.0
        if raw_average < 0:
            signal = -1
            self.cont2cgi_dict['status']=-1
        else:
            self.temperature = self.m*raw_average+self.c

        setpoint = int(self.cgi2cont_dict['setpoint'])
        hyst = int(self.cgi2cont_dict['hysteresis'])
        flag = int(self.cgi2cont_dict['enable'])
        if flag:
            self.cont2cgi_dict['enabled']=True
        else:
            self.cont2cgi_dict['enabled']=False


        if flag and setpoint-hyst > self.temperature:
            self.devices[0].pin_on(32)
            self.cont2cgi_dict['drive_on']=True
        if flag == False or self.temperature > setpoint:
```

```
        self.devices[0].pin_off(32)
        self.cont2cgi_dict['drive_on']=False

    self.cont2cgi_dict['time_stamp']=time()
interf1=DeviceB('FTCVMOYU')
cont1=Cont([interf1])
draw1=BmpDraw('../htdocs/images/display1_tem.bmp')
while 1:
    cont1.read_temp()
    t='%0.02f' % (cont1.temperature)

    f=open('cont2cgi','w')
    pickle.dump(cont1.cont2cgi_dict, f)
    f.close()
    try:
        f = open('cgi2cont','r')
        cgi2cont_cx=pickle.load(f)
        for key in cgi2cont_cx.keys():
            cont1.cgi2cont_dict[key]=cgi2cont_cx[key]

        f.close()
    except:
        pass
    s=int(cont1.cgi2cont_dict['setpoint'])
    h=int(cont1.cgi2cont_dict['hysteresis'])
    if draw1.flag==1:
        draw1.read_template()
        x=5
        ay=46
        for n in range(0,10):
            ax=x+n
            bx=ax
            by=127+8*cont1.temperature
            draw1.line(ax,ay,bx,by,[0,0,255])

        ax = 19
        bx = 36
        ay = 127+s*8
        by = ay
        draw1.line(ax,ay,bx,by,[0,255,255])
        ay = ay-h*8
        by = ay
        draw1.line(ax,ay,bx,by,[0,255,255])
```

```
draw1.write_file('../htdocs/images/display1.bmp')

print cont1.cgi2cont_dict
print cont1.cont2cgi_dict
print
```

Prog 10 – 3 Part 4 (controller.py)

10.5 Internet Access

Chapter 8 showed how to access the apache server by using an ad-hoc network or your Wi-Fi LAN. There is nothing stopping you from accessing externally over the Internet. The computer that you are running the server and the hardware interface on needs to be on the LAN. It is possible to do it via an ad-hoc network but this is beyond the scope of this book as it involves something called port forwarding. For example, to set up a BT Home Hub (common in the UK) follow these instructions. The manual for your particular router will give you the information you need.

- Access the home hub through a web browser at 192.168.1.254
- Go to "Advanced" you have to log in.
- Under "Configuration" got to "Application Sharing" and on the drop down menu for "Game or Application choose "HTTP Server (World Wide Web)". On the "Device" drop down menu choose "<user -defined...>". Enter the LAN IP address of the computer with apache server.
- Click "Add"
- Go to "Internet" under "Configuration" and find your current IP address on the Internet. Or visit "http://www.ip-adress.com" (that is how they spell it) to get it.
- Enter this IP address in the address bar of your browser and if you can see your apache server you are on the Internet.

The big draw back is that with a dynamic IP address on the Internet, it will change from time to time and you can not guarantee access. You can however sign to one of the Dynamic DNS providers if this of interest to you.

Chapter 11

Producing a Your Own Customized Linux Disk

11.1 Introduction

This final chapter will show you how to customize a Slax CD. It will cover adding your own projects, how to make applications start automatically, how to automatically copy files at start up and shut down. The really good thing about live distributions on CDs is that they are portable and you cannot accidentally corrupt them they always boot up to the same state. You are not limited to booting from a CD if your computer has the option to boot from a USB memory stick; the operating system can be put on one of those. There will also be instructions on compiling Python, Tkinter and other applications from source so you can take a basic Slax disk and update in the future.

11.2 Adding An Icon For Your Software

Having developed your Tkinter project it would be better to have it visible on the desktop and be able to start it by clicking on an icon. The first thing to do is to put the program file in a directory such as "/root" or a subdirectory of it. Then check that the first line of the Python program is "#!usr/local/bin/python". I will use "prog_07_06.py" as an example. Ensure that any Python modules that contain classes that are needed such as "interface_classes.py" are also copied to this directory, or to "/usr/local/lib/python/".

```
#!/usr/local/bin/python
#prog_07_06.py
from interface_classes import *
from pickle  import *
from time import *
…......................
…........................
```

The program file permissions have to be set to make it executable by navigating to the directory that holds the program and using "chmod 755 prog_07_06.py", see chapter 1 about file permissions. For an icon you will need an image, a square is best but it can be anything you like. Just copy it to a suitable directory, the one the program is in is probably best.

To create the icon follow the following steps.
- Right click on the desktop.
- Select "Create New"
- Select "Link to Application"
- Type in the text box the name you want to use, say "Temperature Controller"
- Click on the "gear wheel" icon and then the "Other icons" radio button.
- Click on "Browse" and navigate to your image file then select "open"
- Select "Permissions" tab and select "Is executable" box.
- Select "Application" tab and then use the "Browse" button to navigate to the program file, then click open.
- Finally click "Ok

The icon on the desktop should be able to launch the program

11.3 Making a Live Linux Disk

The way I am going to describe will take the operating system as it is once you have added your own software -and having made any changes to say the wallpaper or Firefox settings that you prefer- to make a bootable disk that will always start from this configuration. The method will use the "Linux Live scripts" which are available at "http://www.linux-live.org/" they have already been downloaded and are in the directory "/root/live_linux_scripts" in a compressed form in the file "linux-live-6.3.0.tar.gz".

You will need a USB memory stick or external hard drive, 1 Gbyte will be plenty as this will end up holding a compressed file system and an image of the final CD. Follow the instruction list below.

- Get your operating system the way you want it with the applications you have written and setting up desktop icons as described above. Everything has to be in live RAM file system.
- Plug in the USB memory stick that is going to be used to assemble your distribution.
- When the KDE Daemon window pops up click "OK" and make a note of the path it will be something like "system:/media/sda1" where "./sda1" will depend on your computer.
- You can use "df -h" to list all you drives giving the sizes in Mbytes or Gbytes as a

way of identifying them.

- Open a console window, everything will be done at the command line.
- Change directory to "/tmp" with "cd /tmp"
- Using " tar xvf /root/live_linux_scripts/linux-live-6.3.0.tar.gz" uncompress the Live Linux Scripts to this directory. You will see the contents of this tar file opened into a directory "linux-live-6.3.0/"
- Change directory to "/tmp/linux-live-6.3.0/" with "cd linux-live-6.3.0/"
- There is a hidden file called ".config" in this directory that needs to have a couple of lines amended. Hidden files start with a dot.
- Type "kate .config" to open the file.
- Change line 9 from 'LIVECDNAME="mylinux" ' to a distinctive name for your CD say "distro1".
- At   line   29   change   "CDDATA=/tmp/live_data_$$"   to "CDDATA=/mnt/sda1/tmp/live_data_$$".
- Save the amended ".config" file and then in the dropdown file menu in kate click on "Close All", if you don't do this then kate will be forever trying to open any files you have open here on the new CD.
- To start the process of creating the compressed file system, and a few other files that will be needed to make the CD image type "./build", you will prompted for the name of your live distro, just press enter, you will also be prompted for the name of the kernel again just press enter.
- The build process will take a while.
- There might be an error message saying that there is no free loop device, if this happens follow this sub-list.
    - Change directory with "cd /dev"
    - List the loop devices with "ls loop*"
    - Pick a number that is not there, suppose "loop12" is not there
    - Create a loop device with "mknod loop12 b 7 12". Note the 7 and the 12, it has to be 7 and 12 is the number I chose.
    - Change directory to your memory stick with "cd /mnt/sda1/tmp"
    - Delete everything in this directory as it won't be needed with "rm -r *, they are the remains of the false start"
    - Change directory to "/tmp" with "cd /tmp"
    - Try "./build" again.
- When the build is complete there will be a message, ignore this as there is more to do yet, so just press enter.
- Change directory to your CD ROM with "cd /mnt/hdd/boot".

- Using " cp -r slax.cfg slax.png isolinux/ /mnt/sda1/tmp/live_data_24236/boot/" copy these two files and the directory to your new file system, note the number "24236" will be different for you but the auto-complete using the tab key will find it for you. The reason you have to do this is so that Slax will boot up with the splash screen and boot options. Otherwise the new CD will just boot up to the command line requiring the X server that handles the graphics display to be started manually.
- Using "cd /mnt/sdd1/tmp/live_data_24236/distro1/" change directory.
- Type "./make_iso.sh ../../Slax_custom1.iso" to create the bootable CD image. Which will be in the "mnt/sda1/tmp/" directory.

11.4 Free-ing Up the CDROM Drive

When you boot Slax up from a CD there is a boot option "Slax Copy To RAM" as long as your computer has enough RAM, 500 Mbytes should be enough, the whole operating system will be loaded into RAM and the CD ejected. This does two things, one the CD ROM drive is now available to burn CDs and two, you will notice things work more quickly. To burn your new image insert a blank writable CD and choose "K3b", to burn the CD image from your memory stick. Reboot the computer and see if your own customized distro works.

11.5 Minor Amendments to a Distro

Creating the compressed file system using the Live Linux Scripts is time consuming. If you only want to make a small alteration there is a facility that allows directories and files to be added at boot time. Suppose you have written a new control application called "regulator.py" and have it all working with "regulator.py in the "/root" directory you have created an icon on the desktop and called the application at the icon "Regulator". The list below describes how to make small amendments. If you have not used the Linux Live scripts to create a compressed file system you can just copy recursively the two directories from the CD to a USB memory stick and use that.

- At the command line use cd /mnt/sda1/tmp/live_data_24236/distro1/rootcopy/" to change directory to the "rootycopy" directory, obviously changing this command to suit your setup.
- The contents of the "rootcopy" directory get copied to the file sytem of the live operating system at boot time, you have to create any directories here to mirror the directories that are to be copied to. Using "mkdir root" and then "mkdir root/Desktop"
- Use "cp /root/Desktop/Regulator.desktop /mnt/sdd1/tmp/live_data_24236/distro1/rootcopy/root/Desktop/" to copy the icon file.
- Use "cp /root/regulator.py /mnt/sda1/tmp/live_data_24236/distro1/rootcopy/root/" to copy the program file. Also copy any other files such as "interface_classes.py" if they are needed and the image file for the icon if you have one.
- Now to create another CD image, change directory with "cd /mnt/sda1/tmp/live_data_24236/distro1"
- Create your CD image with "./make_iso.sh ../../Slax_distro1.iso" which will be in the "/mnt/sda1/tmp" directory.
- From this image you can burn another CD with this small amendment included.

11.6 Automation

You might want certain programs to run automatically when the computer boots up. Depending on what type of program you want run there are two choices where you can put the instructions; if its a graphical program that needs the X server then you have to create a "bash" script in the directory "/root/.kde/Autostart". Executable files in this directory get run when the desktop session starts. This will have to be part of your amended distro either by using the rootcopy method or by the Linux Live Scripts method. Prog 11 – 1 shows "Autostart" amended to automatically start the apache web server, the program "regulator.py" and kate the text editor when the computer boots up.

```
#!bin/sh
kate &
/usr/local/apache2/bin/apachectl start
cd /root
./regulator.py &
```

       Prog 11 – 1

The reason for the ampersand after "kate" and "./regulator.py" is to allow the script to start more than one program. If they weren't there the script would stop, waiting for kate to be closed. Starting apache does not need this.

The alternative place to put commands to be carried out on boot up is in the file "/etc/rc.d/rc.local". You simply add any command line commands and then make the file executable with "chmod 755 rc.local". This is only for non-graphical programs such as copying files or Python programs that do not require Tkinter.

If you want to save files from directories that are in RAM such as the "/root" directory you can create a script in "/etc/rc.d" called "rc.local_shutdown"; Prog 11 – 2 shows this. Prog 11 -3 is the script to copy the files back up on boot up, do not forget to "chmod" to make it executable.

```
#!/bin/sh
cp -r /root  /mnt/sda1
```

Prog 11 – 2

Again remember this will have to be incorporated in an amended distibution if you want it to always happen

```
#!/bin/sh
#
# /etc/rc.d/rc.local:  Local system initialization script.
#
# Put any local startup commands in here.  Also, if you have
# anything that needs to be run at shutdown time you can
# make an /etc/rc.d/rc.local_shutdown script and put those
# commands in there.

cp -r /mnt/sda1/root  /
```

Prog 11 – 3

11.7 Compiling Applications From Source

The standard Slax distribution does not have Python installed. If in the future you upgrade to a newer version of Slax or perhaps a permanent installation of Linux, Slackware is a good choice and then you will need to install Python and Tkinter from source. The first thing you need is the source code that can be obtained on the internet, the source files used here are "Python-2.6.4.tgz", "tcl8.5.7-src.tar.gz", and tk8.5.7-src.tar.gz. The following list explains how to proceed.

- Copy the source files to "/root"
- Use "tar xvf   tcl8.5.7-src.tar.gz"
- Change directory with " cd tcl8.5.7/unix/"
- Run the program "configure" with "./configure" then wait for it to complete.
- Run the program "make" with "make" and wait for it to complete.
- Run "make install" and wait for it to complete.
- Change directory to "/root"
- Use "tar xvf tk8.5.7-src.tar.gz"
- Change directory with "cd tk8.5.7/unix/"
- Run the program "configure" with "./configure" then wait for it to complete.
- Run the program "make" with "make" and wait for it to complete.
- Run "make install" and wait for it to complete.
- If you want to you can run a series of tests with "make test" to see Tk working.
- Change directory to "/root"
- Use "tar xvf Python-2.6.4.tgz"
- Open the file "/root/Python-2.6.4/Modules/Setup.dist" with kate
- Scroll down to the line "# The _tkinter module." and amend the lines as shown. I have indicated where I have made changes with "<<<<"

The _tkinter module.
#
The command for _tkinter is long and site specific. Please
uncomment and/or edit those parts as indicated. If you don't have a
specific extension (e.g. Tix or BLT), leave the corresponding line
commented out. (Leave the trailing backslashes in! If you
experience strange errors, you may want to join all uncommented
lines and remove the backslashes -- the backslash interpretation is
done by the shell's "read" command and it may not be implemented on
every system.

```
# *** Always uncomment this (leave the leading underscore in!):    <<<<
_tkinter _tkinter.c tkappinit.c -DWITH_APPINIT \
# *** Uncomment and edit to reflect where your Tcl/Tk libraries are:    <<<<
        -L/usr/local/lib \
# *** Uncomment and edit to reflect where your Tcl/Tk headers are:    <<<<
        -I/usr/local/include \
# *** Uncomment and edit to reflect where your X11 header files are:    <<<<
        -I/usr/X11R6/include \
# *** Or uncomment this for Solaris:
#        -I/usr/openwin/include \
# *** Uncomment and edit for Tix extension only:
#        -DWITH_TIX -ltix8.1.8.2 \
# *** Uncomment and edit for BLT extension only:
#        -DWITH_BLT -I/usr/local/blt/blt8.0-unoff/include -lBLT8.0 \
# *** Uncomment and edit for PIL (TkImaging) extension only:
#    (See http://www.pythonware.com/products/pil/ for more info)
#        -DWITH_PIL -I../Extensions/Imaging/libImaging tkImaging.c \
# *** Uncomment and edit for TOGL extension only:
#        -DWITH_TOGL togl.c \
# *** Uncomment and edit to reflect your Tcl/Tk versions:    <<<<
        -ltk8.5 -ltcl8.5 \
# *** Uncomment and edit to reflect where your X11 libraries are:    <<<<
        -L/usr/X11R6/lib \
# *** Or uncomment this for Solaris:
#        -L/usr/openwin/lib \
# *** Uncomment these for TOGL extension only:
#        -lGL -lGLU -lXext -lXmu \
# *** Uncomment for AIX:
#        -lld \
# *** Always uncomment this; X11 libraries to link with:    <<<<
        -lX1
```

- Save the amended file as "Setup", yes "Setup" not "Setup.dist".
- Change directory to "/root/Python-2.6.4".
- At the command line type "export LD_RUN_PATH=/usr/local/lib" .
- Run the program "configure" with "./configure" then wait for it to complete.
- Run the program "make" with "make" and wait for it to complete.
- Run "make install" and wait for it to complete.

You should now have Python and Tkinter installed. In order to use the FTDI interface the next thing is to compile from source libftdi, this can be downloaded from the internet the version used here is "libftdi-0.17.tar.gz". The procedure is the same as before.

- Uncompress the source file with "tar xvf libftdi-0.17.tar.gz".
- Change directory with "cd /root/ libftdi-0.17"
- Use "./configure"
- Use "make"
- Use "make install"

The Python library "_simple_ftdi.so" needs to be copied to "/usr/local/lib/python2.6. You can get that from the book's downloadable CD in the "/root/book/swig" directory or "/usr/local/lib/python2.6". Once everything is installed you can delete all the source code unless you want to keep it in your new distribution.

Lastly the apache web server needs to be obtained and installed. Its installation is straightforward and just needs to be un-tared then "configure, make, make install". The way it comes configured will work fine.

11.8 Using a Bootable USB Memory Stick

Slax or any live distribution you create with the Linux Live Scripts can be run from a USB Memory stick. All you have to do is copy recursively the directories from the CD or the ones in the "live_data_24236/" directory onto a memory stick and then proceed as follows.

- Change directory to the "boot" directory on the memory stick.
- Run the program "bootinst.sh" with "./bootinst.sh"

Now you have to get your computer to boot from the USB memory stick. This is done by changing your BIOS settings, it will depend on your computer. My own Dell laptop has the option of a one time boot menu by pressing F12 at startup. If you have to alter the bios settings it will be by changing the hard drive order so to make the USB device top of the list.

Using this method has the advantage of freeing the CDROM drive and it also saves changes, but personally I prefer the CD option as it gives you a constant environment. Also when booting from a USB memory stick the system boots up without starting the X server. You have to log in as "root" with password "toor" then using "xconf" to configure the screen followed by "startx" to start the X server.

11.9 A Problem With Firefox

The version of "Firefox 3.5.6",current at the time of writing this book, has a problem on Linux rendering images on some websites. They sometimes appear blacked out or parts of your desktop appears randomly over the web page. The workaround is quite easy, but an inconvenience, but this is what you do.

- Open "/etc/X11/xorg.conf" with "kate" to edit the file
- Find the section "Device" and add this line 'Option "XAANoOffscreenpixmaps" "true" ' before "EndSection"
- Save the file and then use "Ctrl + Alt + Backspace", this will shut down the X server.
- If you are running from a CD the X server will restart with the problem fixed, from a USB device you will need to press return then use "startx"

Alternatively just use "Konqueror" as your web browser.

11.10 Slax Modules

If you visit the Slax website "http://slax.org" there are slax modules of ready compiled applications that you can download. You can either load them when you want any time by using "activate xxxxx.lzm" or you can include the module "xxxxx.lzm" in the modules directory prior creating your own distro.

11.11 Python is Cross Platform

Python as mentioned earlier in the book is cross platform and an interpreter is available for both MS Windows and Mac OS. However the programs in this book being specific to the use of "libftdi" and " _simple_ftdi" are not.

I hope that this book has given you some help and you can see what can be done with just a text editor and some inexpensive hardware. There are drivers available for the FTDI devices for other platforms if you would like to experiment.

Index

A

Abstraction, 23, 24
ad-hoc, 172
analog inputs, 201
analog to digital, 145
apache server, 185, 209
ASCII, 22, 39
assembler, 22

B

bash scripts, 21
binary, 22, 55, 75, 98, 142, 184
binding, 73, 74, 89, 118
BIOS, 10
bit maps, 120
boot, 171, 210
byte, 55

C

calibration, 161
callbacks, 93
canvas, 93
CGI, 184, 194
Character, 18, 22
check buttons, 89, 100
chip select, 145
classes, 63, 75, 140, 156, 210
clock, 145
command line, 162, 173, 195
comparison, 58, 96
compiled, 23, 62
control variable, 98

D

data entry widget, 103
data logger, 156
data types, 27
dictionaries, 47
digital input, 139

digital output, 140, 15

E
elif, 60
else, 60
event driven, 94

F
file permissions, 19
files, 28
Firefox, 19, 171, 180, 211, 219
floats, 27
forms, 190, 194
functions, 49, 150

G
graphic user interface, 184
grid layout, 90

H
Hexadecimal, 105, 174
history, 15
html, 90, 171, 184
hysteresis, 68, 169, 202

I
Idle, 26
import, 51
inheritance, 63, 68
instances, 63
integers, 27, 81, 98, 106
interactive prompt, 26, 51
Internet, 51, 171, 209
interpreted, 23, 27, 59, 123
IP address, 171, 172

J
junk bytes, 133

K
kate, 15, 171, 212

L
LAN, 172, 209
linux, 10, 19, 173, 183, 210
lists, 42
logic, 54

M
machine code, 22

N
networks, 120, 173

O
object oriented63, 156
objects, 27, 42, 61
operator overloading, 29
opto-isolator, 153

P
persistance, 61
pickle, 61, 169, 198, 210

Q

R
radio buttons, 89, 101, 192
redirection, 18
reference voltage, 144, 151, 161
reuasable code, 84, 156
root, 12

S
scale, 96, 129, 156
sensor, 152, 158
server side code, 185, 194
setpoint, 63, 169, 202

simple_ftdi (_simple_ftdi), 72, 95, 116, 143, 150, 218
strings, 28, 40, 98, 12
struct, 123
switch de-bounce, 80

T
table layout, 187
tables, 55
temperature, 152, 156, 158, 202
time, 11, 23, 51, 72, 109, 130, 154, 171, 198, 219
Tkinter, 89, 93, 120, 187, 210
tuples, ,48, 123

U
UM245R, 71, 139, 144, 156, 164

V
voltage, 22, 3, 68, 80, 144, 151

W
watchdog circuit, 154
Wi-Fi, 172, 209
widget, 89, 96, 103, 118, 192
wild cards, 18

X
X server, 21

Y